Lecture Notes in Computer Science 13729

More information about this series at https://link.springer.com/bookseries/558

Xiuqin Pan · Ting Jin · Liang-Jie Zhang (Eds.)

Artificial Intelligence and Mobile Services – AIMS 2022

11th International Conference
Held as Part of the Services Conference Federation, SCF 2022
Honolulu, HI, USA, December 10–14, 2022
Proceedings

Editors
Xiuqin Pan
Minzu University of China
Beijing, China

Ting Jin
Hainan University
Haikou, China

Liang-Jie Zhang ⓘD
Kingdee International Software
Group Co., Ltd.
Shenzhen, China

ISSN 0302-9743   ISSN 1611-3349 (electronic)
Lecture Notes in Computer Science
ISBN 978-3-031-23503-0   ISBN 978-3-031-23504-7 (eBook)
https://doi.org/10.1007/978-3-031-23504-7

This Springer imprint is published by the registered company Springer Nature Switzerland AG
The registered company address is: Gewerbestrasse 11, 6330 Cham, Switzerland

Preface

The 2022 International Conference on AI & Mobile Services (AIMS 2022) was an international forum dedicated to exploring different aspects of AI (from technologies to approaches and algorithms) and mobile services (from business management to computing systems, algorithms, and applications) and to promoting technological innovations in research and development of mobile services, including, but not limited to, wireless and sensor networks, mobile and wearable computing, mobile enterprise and eCommerce, ubiquitous collaborative and social services, machine-to-machine and Internet-of-Things clouds, cyber-physical integration, and big data analytics for mobility-enabled services.

AIMS 2022 was one of the events of the Services Conference Federation event (SCF 2022), which had the following 10 collocated service-oriented sister conferences: the International Conference on Web Services (ICWS 2022), the International Conference on Cloud Computing (CLOUD 2022), the International Conference on Services Computing (SCC 2022), the International Conference on Big Data (BigData 2022), the International Conference on AI & Mobile Services (AIMS 2022), the International Conference on Metaverse (METAVERSE 2022), the International Conference on Internet of Things (ICIOT 2022), the International Conference on Cognitive Computing (ICCC 2022), the International Conference on Edge Computing (EDGE 2022), and the International Conference on Blockchain (ICBC 2022).

This volume presents the papers accepted at AIMS 2022. Its major topics included AI Modeling, AI Analysis, AI and Mobile Applications, AI Architecture, AI Management, AI Engineering, Mobile Backend as a Service (MBaaS), User Experience of AI, and Mobile Services.

We accepted 10 full papers. Each was reviewed and selected by two independent members of the Program Committee. We are pleased to thank the authors whose submissions and participation made this conference possible. We also want to express our thanks to the Program Committee members, for their dedication in helping to organize the conference and review the submissions.

December 2022

Xiuqin Pan
Ting Jin
Liang-Jie Zhang

Organization

Services Conference Federation (SCF 2022)

General Chairs

Ali Arsanjani   Google, USA
Wu Chou   Essenlix, USA

Coordinating Program Chair

Liang-Jie Zhang   Kingdee International Software Group, China

CFO and International Affairs Chair

Min Luo   Georgia Tech, USA

Operations Committee

Jing Zeng   China Gridcom, China
Yishuang Ning   Tsinghua University, China
Sheng He   Tsinghua University, China

Steering Committee

Calton Pu   Georgia Tech, USA
Liang-Jie Zhang   Kingdee International Software Group, China

AIMS 2022

General Chair

Ruifeng Xu   Harbin Institute of Technology, China

Program Chairs

Xiuqin Pan   Minzu University of China, ChinaJin Ting,
                                       Hainan University, China

Program Committee

Services Society

The Services Society (S2) is a non-profit professional organization that was created to promote worldwide research and technical collaboration in services innovations among academia and industrial professionals. Its members are volunteers from industry and academia with common interests. S2 is registered in the USA as a "501(c) organization", which means that it is an American tax-exempt nonprofit organization. S2 collaborates with other professional organizations to sponsor or co-sponsor conferences and to promote an effective services curriculum in colleges and universities. S2 initiates and promotes a "Services University" program worldwide to bridge the gap between industrial needs and university instruction.

The Services Society has formed Special Interest Groups (SIGs) to support technology- and domain-specific professional activities:

- Special Interest Group on Web Services (SIG-WS)
- Special Interest Group on Services Computing (SIG-SC)
- Special Interest Group on Services Industry (SIG-SI)
- Special Interest Group on Big Data (SIG-BD)
- Special Interest Group on Cloud Computing (SIG-CLOUD)
- Special Interest Group on Artificial Intelligence (SIG-AI)
- Special Interest Group on Edge Computing (SIG-EC)
- Special Interest Group on Cognitive Computing (SIG-CC)
- Special Interest Group on Blockchain (SIG-BC)
- Special Interest Group on Internet of Things (SIG-IOT)
- Special Interest Group on Metaverse (SIG-Metaverse)

Services Conference Federation (SCF)

As the founding member of SCF, the first International Conference on Web Services (ICWS) was held in June 2003 in Las Vegas, USA. The First International Conference on Web Services - Europe 2003 (ICWS-Europe'03) was held in Germany in October 2003. ICWS-Europe'03 was an extended event of the 2003 International Conference on Web Services (ICWS 2003) in Europe. In 2004 ICWS-Europe changed to the European Conference on Web Services (ECOWS), which was held in Erfurt, Germany.

SCF 2019 was held successfully during June 25–30, 2019 in San Diego, USA. Affected by COVID-19, SCF 2020 was held online successfully during September 18–20, 2020, and SCF 2021 was held virtually during December 10–14, 2021.

Celebrating its 20-year birthday, the 2022 Services Conference Federation (SCF 2022, www.icws.org) was a hybrid conference with a physical onsite in Honolulu, Hawaii, USA, satellite sessions in Shenzhen, Guangdong, China, and also online sessions for those who could not attend onsite. All virtual conference presentations were given via prerecorded videos in December 10–14, 2022 through the BigMarker Video Broadcasting Platform: https://www.bigmarker.com/series/services-conference-federati/series_summit.

Just like SCF 2022, SCF 2023 will most likely be a hybrid conference with physical onsite and virtual sessions online, it will be held in September 2023.

To present a new format and to improve the impact of the conference, we are also planning an Automatic Webinar which will be presented by experts in various fields. All the invited talks will be given via prerecorded videos and will be broadcast in a live-like format recursively by two session channels during the conference period. Each invited talk will be converted into an on-demand webinar right after the conference.

In the past 19 years, the ICWS community has expanded from Web engineering innovations to scientific research for the whole services industry. Service delivery platforms have been expanded to mobile platforms, the Internet of Things, cloud computing, and edge computing. The services ecosystem has been enabled gradually, with value added and intelligence embedded through enabling technologies such as Big Data, artificial intelligence, and cognitive computing. In the coming years, all transactions involving multiple parties will be transformed to blockchain.

Based on technology trends and best practices in the field, the Services Conference Federation (SCF) will continue to serve as a forum for all services-related conferences. SCF 2022 defined the future of the new ABCDE (AI, Blockchain, Cloud, Big Data & IOT). We are very proud to announce that SCF 2023's 10 colocated theme topic conferences will all center around "services", while each will focus on exploring different themes (Web-based services, cloud-based services, Big Data-based services, services innovation lifecycles, AI-driven ubiquitous services, blockchain-driven trust service ecosystems, Metaverse services and applications, and emerging service-oriented technologies).

The 10 colocated SCF 2023 conferences will be sponsored by the Services Society, the world-leading not-for-profit organization dedicated to serving more than 30,000 services computing researchers and practitioners worldwide. A bigger platform means bigger opportunities for all volunteers, authors, and participants. Meanwhile, Springer will provide sponsorship for Best Paper Awards. All 10 conference proceedings of SCF 2023 will be published by Springer, and to date the SCF proceedings have been indexed in the ISI Conference Proceedings Citation Index (included in the Web of Science), the Engineering Index EI (Compendex and Inspec databases), DBLP, Google Scholar, IO-Port, MathSciNet, Scopus, and ZbMath.

SCF 2023 will continue to leverage the invented Conference Blockchain Model (CBM) to innovate the organizing practices for all 10 conferences. Senior researchers in the field are welcome to submit proposals to serve as CBM ambassadors for individual conferences.

SCF 2023 Events

The 2023 edition of the Services Conference Federation (SCF) will include 10 service-oriented conferences: ICWS, CLOUD, SCC, BigData, AIMS, METAVERSE, ICIOT, EDGE, ICCC and ICBC.

The 2023 International Conference on Web Services (ICWS 2023, http://icws.org/2023) will be the flagship theme-topic conference for Web-centric services, enabling technologies and applications.

The 2023 International Conference on Cloud Computing (CLOUD 2023, http://thecloudcomputing.org/2023) will be the flagship theme-topic conference for resource sharing, utility-like usage models, IaaS, PaaS, and SaaS.

The 2023 International Conference on Big Data (BigData 2023, http://bigdatacongress.org/2023) will be the theme-topic conference for data sourcing, data processing, data analysis, data-driven decision-making, and data-centric applications.

The 2023 International Conference on Services Computing (SCC 2023, http://thescc.org/2023) will be the flagship theme-topic conference for leveraging the latest computing technologies to design, develop, deploy, operate, manage, modernize, and redesign business services.

The 2023 International Conference on AI & Mobile Services (AIMS 2023, http://ai1000.org/2023) will be a theme-topic conference for artificial intelligence, neural networks, machine learning, training data sets, AI scenarios, AI delivery channels, and AI supporting infrastructures, as well as mobile Internet services. AIMS will bring AI to mobile devices and other channels.

The 2023 International Conference on Metaverse (Metaverse 2023, http://www.metaverse1000.org/2023) will focus on innovations of the services industry, including financial services, education services, transportation services, energy services, government services, manufacturing services, consulting services, and other industry services.

The 2023 International Conference on Cognitive Computing (ICCC 2023, http://thecognitivecomputing.org/2023) will focus on leveraging the latest computing technologies to simulate, model, implement, and realize cognitive sensing and brain operating systems.

The 2023 International Conference on Internet of Things (ICIOT 2023, http://iciot.org/2023) will focus on the science, technology, and applications of IOT device innovations as well as IOT services in various solution scenarios.

The 2023 International Conference on Edge Computing (EDGE 2023, http://the edgecomputing.org/2023) will be a theme-topic conference for leveraging the latest computing technologies to enable localized device connections, edge gateways, edge applications, edge-cloud interactions, edge-user experiences, and edge business models.

The 2023 International Conference on Blockchain (ICBC 2023, http://blockc hain1000.org/2023) will concentrate on all aspects of blockchain, including digital currencies, distributed application development, industry-specific blockchains, public blockchains, community blockchains, private blockchains, blockchain-based services, and enabling technologies.

Contents

Research Track

Push-Based Forwarding Scheme Using Fuzzy Logic to Mitigate the Broadcasting Storm Effect in VNDN

Sajjad Ahmad Khan🄙 and Huhnkuk Lim(✉)🄙

Department of Computer Engineering, Hoseo University, Asan-si, South Korea
slow63347@gmail.com

Abstract. Vehicular Named Data Networking (VNDN) is one of the potential and future networking architectures that could allow smart vehicles to exchange data by simply disseminating the content over the network. VNDN supports only a pull-based data forwarding model. In the pull-based mode, the content is forwarded upon request. However, in critical situations, a push-based data forwarding model is essential to design in order to broadcast the critical data packets without any requests. One of the major challenges of push-based data forwarding in VNDN is the broadcast storm effect, which occurs when a producer broadcasts critical information over the network. For instance, in emergency situations such as accidents, road hazards, rain, etc., the producer generates a critical data packet and broadcasts it to all the nearby vehicles. Subsequently, every vehicle broadcasts the same critical data packet to each other, which leads to the broadcast storm effect on the network. Therefore, this paper proposes a Fuzzy logic-based scheme to mitigate the broadcast storm effect. The novelty of this paper is the suggestion and application of a Fuzzy logic approach in order to mitigate critical data broadcasting in VNDN. In the proposed scheme, the vehicles are distributed in clusters by using the K-Means clustering algorithm, and then a Cluster Head (CH) is chosen by using a Fuzzy logic approach. The CH is responsible for broadcasting the critical data packets to all other vehicles in a cluster. A Gateway (GW) has the role of forwarding the critical data packets to the nearest clusters via their GWs. The simulation results show that the proposed scheme performs better than the naive scheme in terms of transmitted data packets and efficiency.

Keywords: Push-based forwarding · Critical data packet · Vehicular Named Data Networking (VNDN) · K-means clustering · Fuzzy logic · Cluster Head (CH)

1 Introduction

As smart vehicles enter the commercial market and progress toward full autonomy, and the number of smart vehicles on the road will increase in coming years. Today, smart vehicles such as autonomous vehicles (AVs) and connected

X. Pan et al. (Eds.): AIMS 2022, LNCS 13729, pp. 3–17, 2022.
https://doi.org/10.1007/978-3-031-23504-7_1

cars rely on sensors such as cameras and LiDAR to monitor the roads and drive safely and efficiently [1]. However, if there are other smart vehicles on the road, the vehicles can communicate with one another via a process known as Vehicle-to-Vehicle (V2V) communication. The Intelligent Transportation System (ITS) enables road monitoring, traffic control, vehicular communication, and decision-making in emergence situations, etc., and all these smart vehicles depend on the Vehicular Ad-hoc Network (VANET)'s smooth data delivery [2]. The VANET is based on the traditional Telecommunication Control Protocol (TCP) and Internet Protocol (IP) communication model, which has some limitations when it comes to vehicular communications [3].

On the other hand, Named Data Networking (NDN) is designed under the umbrella of Information Centric Networking (ICN) [4]. NDN is a content-oriented architecture that has the potential to replace IP-based architecture in near future. In the NDN, the data can be accessed according to its name/content/prefix rather than its IP address (host location) [5]. The content's name is a key element for NDN-based communication rather than the IP address. Due to the benefits of NDN over traditional IP-based networking, new designs have been created to implement the VANET by using the NDN architecture. For simplicity, sometimes it refers to Vehicular Named Data Networking (VNDN).

In VNDN, vehicles may be consumers, producers, or intermediate routers. By design, VNDN supports only a pull-based communication model [6]. In pull-based communication, a consumer vehicle creates an interest packet and broadcasts it on the network. The intermediate vehicles forward the interest to other vehicles in the network until it reaches the producer. The producer sends the data packet to the consumer via the same interface that receives the interest [7]. In critical situations such as emergency warnings and accidents, the data must be transmitted in a push-based manner [8]. It means that a producer generates a critical data packet and transmits it to all the vehicles without any request from the consumer. To do so, a push-based data forwarding scheme is required to be designed and modified for the current VNDN forwarding model.

However, the critical data packets are broadcast, creating a broadcast storm effect in the push-based VNDN. To the best of our knowledge, limited work has been done to cope with the above-mentioned issue. The only technique for critical data storm mitigation is presented in [9] for the NDN used for the Internet of Things (IoTs), but not for the VNDN. Therefore, we propose a novel scheme based on a Fuzzy logic approach. This is the first work that we design a Fuzzy logic approach, apply in VNDN and reduce the broadcast storm effect that occurs as a result of the broadcasting of the critical data packet. We assume critical situations, and the critical data packets are transmitted through a push-based mode of communication.

The rest of the paper is structured as follows. Section 2 explains the concept of VNDN. In Sect. 3, the push-based data forwarding in VNDN is explained. The proposed push-based data forwarding scheme with Fuzzy Logic is given in

Sect. 4. Section 5 presents the simulation environment and results. The paper is concluded in Sect. 6.

2 Vehicular Named Data Networking (VNDN)

VNDN is an application class of VANETs and NDN in which a group of vehicles is connected through the On-Board Units (OBUs) and gets access to a centralized data network. An OBU gives vehicles the ability to process, store, and communicate with each other [10]. Additionally, OBUs may link wirelessly to one another with or without Road Side Units (RSUs), enabling them to form ad-hoc, dispersed, and self-organized networks. The major objectives of VANET using the NDN architecture are the exchange of information rigorously and an effort to increase road safety while improving the driving experience. In VNDN, the vehicles can communicate and exchange interest and data packets via V2V and V2RSUs [11]. If a consumer vehicle needs any content, it can generate a request (interest) with the name of the content and broadcast it on the network. The intermediate routers rebroadcast the interest until it reaches the data producer. On the forwarding path, once the interest reaches a node that has the requested data, i.e., the name of the interest is the same as the name of the data or a prefix of the name of the data, the data is sent to the requested consumer vehicle. Since there are no source and destination addresses in a VNDN packet, the intermediate routers use the name and prefix in the Content Store (CS), Pending Interest Table (PIT), and Forwarding Information Base (FIB) to exchange interest and data packets [12].

2.1 Content Store (CS)

A CS is a temporary repository for data packets that the intermediate router receives. In NDN-based communication, the data packets are meaningful and no matter where it comes from or where it is sent, they can be stored in a cache and used later. The old data packet can be replaced by the most recently used data packet. When an intermediate router receives interest, the first check it in its CS.

2.2 Pending Interest Table (PIT)

PITs contain all Interests that have been transmitted by a router but have not yet been fulfilled. Each PIT entry documents the name of the data carried by the Interest and its incoming and outgoing interface(s).

2.3 Forwarding Information Base (FIB)

The FIB generates a routing table that links component names to interfaces. A name-prefix-based routing protocol populates the FIB, which might have many output interfaces for each prefix.

2.4   Consumer Vehicle

In VNDN, any node/vehicle that requests any content or information is called a consumer. Based on this NDN forwarding strategy, a consumer initiates an interest packet and broadcasts it to all the neighboring vehicles. The data packet will be received if the interest is fulfilled by the intermediate routers or the producer. The consumer vehicle is hence the data requester in a VNDN system.

2.5   Producer Vehicle

The node or vehicle that has the original data packet or cache in its depository is the producer in the VNDN. When an interest is received at the producer, a data packet is prepared after matching the name or prefix of the content. The data is then forwarded to the consumer through the same path that the interest packet has traversed.

3   Push-Based Data Forwarding in VNDN

The VNDN basically supports a pull-based architecture in which communication is initiated by a consumer node/vehicle. However, in vehicular communication, there might be some critical situations in which push-based communication should be applied. These critical situations may include the broadcast of traffic information, advertisements, and critical alerts, etc. Figure 1 demonstrates the comparison between the pull-based and push-based data forwarding mechanism in VNDN.

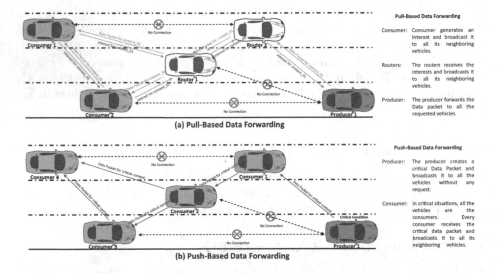

Fig. 1. Comparison of the pull-based and push-based data forwarding in VNDN

A VNDN can be defined as an undirected graph $G_t(V, \in_t)$, where V is the set of vertices and $\in_t$ is the set of links connecting those vehicles at time t. The vehicle set V consists of network vehicles v_1, v_2, v_3, ..., v_N. There is a Producer p producing content and consumer c intended for that content. O is a content object that can be divided into two classes of chunks, the non-critical chunks denoted n_1, n_2, n_3, ..., n_K and the critical chunks denoted r_1, r_2, r_3, ..., r_M. We calculated the total transfer time for the data packet in a pull-based VNDN architecture by using the Eq. 1 [13]. We assume that the size of every chunk regardless of the class is the same and denoted s_r.

$$
\begin{aligned}
T_{TCT}(G_{t\alpha}, G_{tI}, G_{tr}, p, c) = {} & Q(G_{t\alpha}, p, c)t_\alpha + Q(G_{tI}, c, p) \left[\sum_{k=1}^{M} \left(t_y + \frac{S_I}{\tau_y} \right) \right] \\
& + Q(G_{tr}, p, c) \left[\sum_{l=1}^{N} \left(t_x + \frac{S_r}{\tau_x} \right) \right]
\end{aligned}
\tag{1}
$$

where, t_y and τ_y are the latency and transfer rate for interests, and t_x and τ_x be the latency and transfer rate for chunks. $Q(n_1, n_2)$ is the distance between nodes (vehicles). $G_t\alpha$ is the network state at the time the producer advertises content. G_tI is the network state at the time the interest is transmitted. G_tr is the network state at the time the chunk of a critical content is transmitted. S_I and S_r indicate the size of the interest and critical content, respectively. t_α is the time required for a node to transfer a content advertise by a neighbor.

In such push-based communication model, the total transfer time for a critical content can be caluculated using the Eq. 2 [13].

$$
T_{STT}(G_{t\beta}, G_{tr}, p, c) = Q(G_{t\beta}, p, c)t_\beta + Q(G_{tr}, p, c) \left[\sum_{l=1}^{N} \left(t_x + \frac{S_r}{\tau_x} \right) \right]
\tag{2}
$$

where, t_x and τ_x are the latency and transfer rate for the chunks of a critical content. $Q(n_1, n_2)$ is the distance between nodes (vehicles). $G_t\beta$ is the network state at the time producer advertise the critical content. G_tr is the network state at time the chunk of a critical content is transmitted by the producer. S_r indicate the size of the critical content. t_β is the time required for a node to transfer a critical content advertise by a neighbor vehicle.

4 Proposed Push-Based Data Forwarding Scheme with Fuzzy Logic

In order to mitigate the critical data packet broadcast storm, we propose a push-based data forwarding scheme with Fuzzy logic that comprises of several steps.

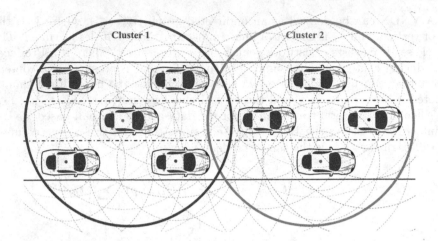

Fig. 2. The proposed K-means clustering method for vehicles clustering in push-based data forwarding in VNDN

4.1   K-Means Clustering

The term clustering can be utilized to manage frequent communication between vehicles. In order to arrange the vehicles into groups, a K-Means clustering approach is employed in this paper. K-Means is a unsupervised machine learning approach that can be used for clustering. It is a technique for automatically dividing the vehicles into clusters or groups. Every vehicle is automatically assigned to a cluster by receiving its Received Signal Strength Indicator (RSSI) value. However, each vehicle belongs to only one cluster. The center value that cluster is called a centroid [14]. At starting, the algorithm takes the number of clusters "K". Then, "K" points are randomly selected for centroids. To find the optimum number of "K", we use an Elbow algorithm.

Based on centroids, the vehicles are grouped together. In the next step, central points are chosen to indicate the new centroids. The vehicles grouped themselves according to the new centroids, and this process keeps continue until no change in the group occurs. The K-Mean algorithm follows the expected maximization to address the problem. After every second, these steps are repeated and allocating the vehicles' locations to the nearest cluster. Each step calculates the a new centroid for each cluster. The normalized function of 'J' is calculated by using Eq. 3. Figure 2 demonstrates the clustering by using the K-Means clustering algorithm.

$$J = \sum_{i=1}^{m} \sum_{k=1}^{K} \omega_{ik} \, |||x_i - \mu_i|||^2 \qquad (3)$$

where $\omega_{ik} = 1$ for data x_i if it belongs to cluster K; otherwise, $\omega_{ik} = 0$. And μ_k is the centroid of each x_i cluster.

On the other hand, the normalized distances from centroids are calculated according to Eq. 4.

$$dist = \sqrt{(x_1 - y_1)^2 + (x_2 - y_2)^2} \tag{4}$$

where x, and y are the coordinates of the each vehicle.

4.2 Selection of Cluster Head (CH) Using Fuzzy Logic

The Fuzzy logic is a strategy that employs more than one parameters to determine and choose one node/vehicle to be the Cluster Head in a cluster. It is the place where the Fuzzy system's membership functions are maintained. The Fuzzy system's rule base is a collection of Fuzzy rules that it will employ to infer. During the fuzzification the input values taken by the Fuzzy system and convert it into the Fuzzy values. Inference System: The Fuzzy output according to the Fuzzy inputs using Fuzzy rules. Defuzzification is converting the resulting Fuzzy output to an actual value [15].

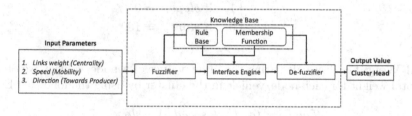

Fig. 3. The Fuzzy logic method used to select the CH

The following input parameters are used to choose the CH in a given cluster. The Fuzzy logic procedure to select a CH is shown in Fig. 3.

Link Weight (Centrality). By selecting the CH in a cluster, the link weight is an important parameter to be considered. During this step, the distances of all nodes/vehicles from the center point is calculated by using the normalized distance Eq. 5.

$$dist_{vi} = \left[norm \left(\sqrt{(x_2 - x_1)^2 + (y_2 - y_1)^2} \right) \right] \times 100 \tag{5}$$

The shortest distance from the center position is given a higher weightage to be chosen as a CH. However, other parameters also impact the selection process.

Speed (Mobility). The speed of a node/vehicle is also an important parameter for selection the CH. If the speed is higher then it means it will move fast and will change it position frequently. Therefore, the speed of a node/vehicle impacts the control system and specially the Fuzzy logic controller. The speed and mobility of a node/vehicles can be calculate by Eq. 6.

$$speed_{vi}(m/s) = \left(\frac{speed_{vi}}{\max_{i=1}^{n} speed} \right) \times 100 \tag{6}$$

The speed of each vehicle vi is normalized by dividing it with the maximum speed of in that cluster. Later, the percentage of all the speed are forwarded to the Fuzzy logic controller.

Direction (Towards Producer). In this step, the direction of the node/vehicle is obtain by taking the slope. If the slope is zero degree then it means the node/vehicle is moving towards the producer of the critical data packet. If the slope is 180°, it indicates that the node/vehicle is moving opposite direction. In this case, the node/vehicle will not be entertained for the selection of CH due to its direction. The Eq. 7 is used for direction of the vehicle.

$$slope_{vi} = \begin{cases} 1, & \text{if } slope_{vi} = 0 \\ 0, & \text{if } slope_{vi} = 180 \end{cases} \tag{7}$$

Total Weight. After calculating the input values of a node/vehicle, we obtain the total weight for each node/vehicle in the cluster by using the following Eq. 8.

$$Total_{vi} = (dist_{vi} + speed_{vi}) \times slope_{vi} \tag{8}$$

$$CH = \min_{i}^{n} (Total_{vi}) \ , \qquad CH \neq 0. \tag{9}$$

Any node/vehicle carrying the minimum value will be selected as the CH of that cluster. It is noteworthy that the value must be greater than zero to participate in the selection process.

4.3   Proposed Data Packet Format

In our push-based data forwarding scheme, we modified the existing data packet format and insert some extra information to be disseminate the critical content. The following extra fields can be inserted to modify/update the data packet in order to control the data broadcasting in the VNDN environment (Table 1).

Alert Type: This is an important field of data packet which can be used to understand the nature of the data packet. In critical scenarios, the alert will be highlighted as critical. Therefore, the consumer vehicles will understand the nature of alert and forward it without having an interest request in their PIT tables.

Table 1. The proposed critical data packet format

Content name
Data
Alert type (critical or normal)
Location
Timer
Signature

Location of the Producer: This field carries the location of the producer when the data packet is generated. By using the location, it helps to find the direction of the critical data packet. The consumer vehicles will be able to take action according to the critical data packet using the location of the producer. In other words, if a the alert is coming on the way of the vehicle, then prior action will be taken, otherwise. it will ignore and drop the alert.

Timer: Timer also plays an important role during the disseminating the data packet in push-based data forwarding. The timer is used to forward the data packet for a specific time. If the timer reach to the maximum time, then the data packet will be dropped and stopped forwarding by the consumer vehicles.

4.4   Proposed Scheme for Producer

Algorithm 1. The proposed push-based critical data forwarding algorithm at a producer

```
 1: Possible events: [Startup, interest i, consumer c, critical content b]
 2: Case Event:
 3: if Producer == New then
 4:     advertise each non-critical content Object O
 5:     if non-critical content i then
 6:         send i to consumer c
 7:         if critical content r then
 8:             construct a critical data packet b
 9:             send critical content b towards CH
10:         end if
11:     end if
12: end if
```

In a critical situation, the push-based data packet is generated by the producer and forward it to the cluster head by using the Algorithm 1. Every vehicle advertises its location, speed and direction to all its neighboring vehicles. During the

Fuzzy logic process, every node/vehicle in the cluster identify the CH and cluster GWs. Therefore, we assume that the producer also belongs to the cluster and have established a connection with CH. When the producer receives a normal interest for normal data packet, it generates the data packet and forwards it to the requested vehicle. However, if there is a critical situation then the producer generates the critical data packet and for forwards it to the CH of that cluster. The CH has the responsibility to broadcast it to all the intermediate vehicles in the clusters. The role of the CH and GW vehicles are presented in Algorithm 2.

4.5   Proposed Scheme for Consumer

In a push-based data forwarding, we assume that all the vehicles are the consumers and the critical information is necessary for them. Therefore, the critical data packet is forwarded to the CH of that cluster without any interest packet request. Once the critical data packet is transmitted to the CH of its cluster. Every consumer vehicle checks its MAC Table, and finds the clustering information. If the consumer vehicle is a CH then it broadcasts the critical data packet to all the member vehicles in the cluster. If the intermediate vehicle is a Gateway (GW) then it forwards it the GW vehicle of its neighbouring cluster. If the consumer vehicle is only a member of that cluster then it drops the data packet and does not forward it to any vehicle in its vicinity. Algorithm 2 describes the role and data forwarding procedures of CH and intermediate vehicles during critical conditions.

Algorithm 2. The proposed push-based critical data forwarding algorithm at a consumer

---

    Received Data Packet: [ID, Content, Alert Type, Location, Timer, Signature]
 2: **if** Alert Type $==b_i$ (critical data packet) **then**
        read b
 4:     **if** Vehicle $(v_i)==$ CH (Cluster Head) **then**
            Broadcast bi
 6:         **if** Vehicle $(v_i)==GW_i$ **then**
                Forward b to GW_{i+1}
 8:         **else**
                drop b
10:         **end if**
        end if
12: **end if**

4.6   Critical Data Forwarding Procedure by the Proposed Scheme

Figure 4 demonstrates the critical data flow from producer to all other vehicles. We assume that the critical data packet such as emergency alert, is necessary for all the vehicle moving towards the location of the of the critical situation. Before any critical condition, all the vehicles are grouped into different clusters by employing the K-Means clusters, discussed in Subsect. 4.1. Subsequently, different roles are assigned to the vehicles in each cluster by using the Fuzzy logic method, presented in Subsect. 4.2.

When there a critical situation occurs, the producer generates a critical data packet and transmits it to the CH by using Algorithm 1. The producer fetch alert type, location, and timer to the critical data packet. Once the data is received by the CH, the critical data packet is broadcasts to all the member vehicles of the clusters. When the critical data packet is receive at the member vehicle of the cluster, it drops the packet. On the other hand, the GW forwards the critical data packet to the next GW of the nearest cluster.

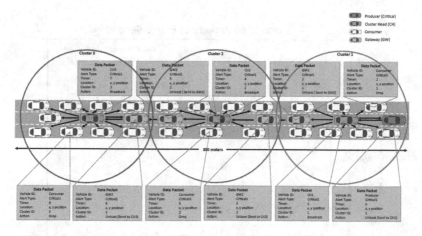

Fig. 4. Example of critical data forwarding scenario by the proposed push based forwarding scheme using Fuzzy logic method

5 Simulation Environment and Results

The NS-3 and ndnSIM tools are used to implement the proposed scheme and analyze the performance. In addition to the traditional NDN structures, Simulation for Urban Mobility (SUMO) was employed to obtain the vehicle movements. For a fair comparison, the simulations employ the same simulation settings, network configuration, Physical and MAC layer parameters, and mobility model. Total 600 vehicle were taken, and were moving with different speeds. The observed area were taken from 300 m and a three lane road were considered. The remaining simulation settings are listed in Table 2.

In addition, a random number of critical vehicles are dispersed evenly over the network, and each vehicle randomly creates a critical data packet for the period of the experiment. Every car communicates its location with its neighbors through

Table 2. The simulation parameters and their values

Parameter	Value
Network model	NS-3 and ndnSIM
Mobility model	SUMO
Number of vehicles	600
Vehicle speed	30–100 KM/H
Transmission mode	V2V (IEEE 802.11p)

critical data packet. Each forwarder disables content caching; nevertheless, when a consumer node gets the desired Data, it caches it in its CS.

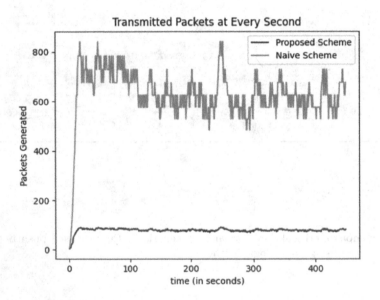

Fig. 5. Total number of packets vs. time in seconds

Figure 5 shows the total number of critical data packets are transmitted over each iteration with respect to the number of vehicles. We can observe that the naive scheme transmits huge number of critical data packets while the Proposed scheme transmits less number of critical data packets. In the naive scheme, all the vehicles broadcasts the receive critical data packet. Hence, every vehicle receives multiple copies of the same critical data packet. On the other hand, the proposed scheme allows CH only to broadcasts the critical data packet to all its member vehicles.

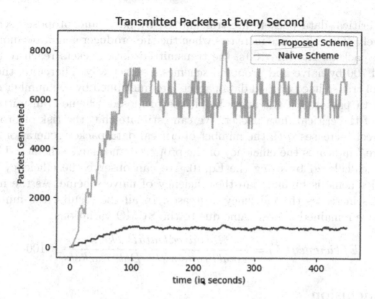

Fig. 6. Total number of packets vs. time in seconds

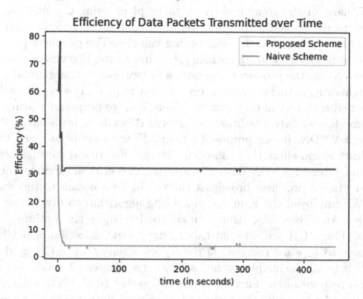

Fig. 7. Efficiency in percentage

In Fig. 6, we can observe that the total number of critical data packets generated and transmitted with respect to time. Also, the number of vehicles are varying with respect to time. At start, only one critical data packet is generated and transmitted. At time 10 s, two critical data packets are generated and transmitted using naive and proposed schemes. We can see that almost 1800 and 200 critical data packets are transmitted by naive and proposed schemes, respectively. The difference increases when the the producer generates more critical data packets. At time 100 s, the transmitted data packets reach to almost 7000 and 700 by naive and proposed schemes, respectively. Therefore, the total number of transmitted critical data packets are multiplied by the number of generated data packet. On the other hand, the proposed scheme transmitted less number of the critical data packet. We can estimate that the risk of broadcast storm effect increases with the number of critical data packet generation.

Figure 7 indicates the efficiency of the proposed and naive schemes. The efficiency is calculated by using the Eq. 10. We can observe the efficiency of the proposed scheme is higher than the efficiency of naive scheme. As the number of vehicles increases the efficiency decreases. In all the results, the number of vehicles are remained almost same due to the SUMO variations.

$$Efficiency\,(\%) = \frac{RequiredDataPackets}{TotalTransmittedDataPackets} \times 100 \qquad (10)$$

6   Conclusion

In VNDN, most of the content delivery takes place using the pull-based communication model. When a consumer requires content, it generates an interest request and broadcasts it to the neighboring vehicles. The producer provides the content to the requested consumers using the same route. Likewise, in push-based forwarding VNDN, the producer generates a critical content and broadcasts it to all the neighboring vehicles without any interest request, however, it will create a broadcast storm effect in the network. Therefore, we proposed a using a Fuzzy logic scheme to mitigate the broadcast storm effect in a push-based data forwarding in a VNDN. In our proposed scheme, Fuzzy logic is designed to reduce the broadcast storm effect that can occur during the critical data packet broadcast in a push-based VNDN data forwarding. The critical circumstances were considered when a producer broadcast the useful information to the rest of the vehicles. We employed the K-means clustering algorithm to divide the vehicles into groups. An Elbow algorithm is used to determine the optimum number of clusters. Then, CH are selected using Fuzzy logic. Election of a CH makes the producer to forward the critical data packet only to the CH, and the CH broadcasts it to all the member vehicles inside the clusters. In addition, the GW vehicles are responsible to forwards the data packet to the GW vehicles of the next vehicles. As a result, the transmitted critical data packets are mitigated efficiently. The results show that the proposed scheme transmitted less number of data packets and reduce the chances of broadcast storm in the VNDN environment. We also presented that the efficiency of the proposed is higher than the naive method.

Acknowledgement. This work was sponsored by the Korean Government (Ministry of Science and ICT) through the National Research Foundation of Korea (NRF) under a Grant number 2021R1A2C1010481.

References

1. Al-Omaisi, H., Sundararajan, E.A., Alsaqour, R., Abdullah, N.F., Abdelhaq, M.: A survey of data dissemination schemes in vehicular named data networking. Veh. Commun. **30** (2021)
2. Khelifi, H., et al.: Named data networking in vehicular ad hoc networks: state-of-the-art and challenges. IEEE Commun. Surv. Tutor. **22**(1) (2019)
3. Mahmood, J., et al.: Secure message transmission for V2V based on mutual authentication for VANETs. Wirel. Commun. Mob. Comput. **2021** (2021)
4. Lim, H., Ni, A., Kim, D., Ko, Y.-B., Shannigrahi, S., Papadopoulos, C.: NDN construction for big science: lessons learned from establishing a testbed. IEEE Netw. **32**(6) (2018)
5. Shah, P., Kasbe, T.: A review on specification evaluation of broadcasting routing protocols in VANET. Comput. Sci. Rev. **41** (2021)
6. Siddiqa, A., Diyan, M., Khan, M.T.R., Saad, M.M., Kim, D.: Mitigating broadcasting storm using multihead nomination clustering in vehicular content centric networks. Electronics **10**(18) (2021)
7. Li, Z., Xu, Y., Zhang, B., Yan, Liu, L.: Packet forwarding in named data networking requirements and survey of solutions. IEEE Commun. Surv. Tutor. **21**(2) (2018)
8. Amadeo, M., Ruggeri, G., Campolo, C., Molinaro, A.: Diversity-improved caching of popular transient contents in vehicular named data networking. Comput. Netw. **184** (2021)
9. Ullah, R., Rehman, M.A.U., Kim, B.S.: Hierarchical name-based mechanism for push-data broadcast control in information-centric multihop wireless networks. Sensors **19**(14) (2019)
10. Duarte, J.M., Braun, T., Villas, L.A.: MobiVNDN: a distributed framework to support mobility in vehicular named-data networking. Ad Hoc Netw. **82** (2019)
11. Ali, I., Lim, H.: NameCent: name centrality-based data broadcast mitigation in vehicular named data networks. IEEE Access **9** (2021)
12. Hannan, A., et al.: Disaster management system aided by named data network of things: architecture, design, and analysis. Sensors **18**(8) (2018)
13. Majeed, M.F., Ahmed, S.H., Dailey, M.N.: Enabling push-based critical data forwarding in vehicular named data networks. IEEE Commun. Lett. **21**(4) (2016)
14. Ayyub, M., Oracevic, A., Hussain, R., Khan, A.A., Zhang, Z.: A comprehensive survey on clustering in vehicular networks: current solutions and future challenges. Ad Hoc Netw. **124** (2022)
15. Chaudhry, S.A., et al.: A lightweight authentication scheme for 6G-IoT enabled maritime transport system. IEEE Trans. Intell. Transp. Syst. (2021)

DCRNNX: Dual-Channel Recurrent Neural Network with Xgboost for Emotion Identification Using Nonspeech Vocalizations

Xingwei Liang[1(✉)], You Zou[1], Tian Xie[2], and Qi Zhou[2]

[1] Konka Corporation, Shenzhen, China
liangxingwei@konka.com
[2] Harbin Institute of Technology (Shenzhen), Shenzhen, China

Abstract. The human voice, especially nonspeech vocalizations, inherently convey emotions. However, existing efforts have ignored such emotional expressions for a long time. Based on this, we propose a Dual-channel Recurrent Neural Network with Xgboost (DCRNNX) to solve emotion recognition using nonspeech vocalizations. The DCRNNX mainly combines two Backbone models. The first model is a two-channel neural network model based on the Deep Neural Network (DNN) and Channel Recurrent Neural Network (CRNN). Channel 1 is constructed by CRNN, and the other model is constructed by Xgboost. Additionally, we employ a smoothing mechanism to integrate the outputs of the two classifiers to promote our DCRNNX. Compared with the baselines, DCRNNX combines not only multiple features but also combines multiple models, which ensures the generalization performance of DCRNNX. Experimental results show that our method achieves 45% and 42% UAR (Unweighted Average Recall), on the development dataset. After model fusion, DCRNNX achieves 46.89% UAR and 37.0% UAR on development and test datasets, respectively. The performance of our method on the development dataset is nearly 6% better than the baselines. Especially, there is a considerable gap between the performance of DCRNNX on the development and the test set. It may be the reason for the differences in emotional characteristics of the male and female voices.

Keywords: Speech emotion recognition · Convolutional recurrent neural network · eXtreme gradient boosting · Model fusion

1 Introduction

Humans express emotions through a variety of vocal channels, including verbal expressions that contain words, sentences, and non-verbal vocal expressions such as interjections. At present, many works on emotion recognition in acoustics have been devoted to the study of emotions expressed in language, while the research on emotion recognition of non-verbal expressions has yet to be developed.

However, Non-verbal vocal expressions play an important role in many applications, especially in today's increasingly common human-computer interaction systems. Correctly understanding the emotions embedded in non-verbal vocal expressions is essential for the purposes such as intelligent healthcare and psychological counseling.

In this paper, we built a speech emotion recognition system to predict emotion contained in non-verbal speech. The task is first proposed as part of the tasks of the ACM Multimedia 2022 Computational Paralinguistics Challenge [1]. In the field of speech emotion recognition, the Channel Recurrent Neural Network (CRNN) and its variants have been shown to be effective in the field of computational paralinguistics, including keyword discovery [2], speaker recognition [3], and speech emotion recognition [4,5]. However, most of them only focus on using a certain feature as a single-channel input instead of a multi-channel model. Therefore they lack the ability to collect speech emotion information from multiple feature sets. To solve this problem, we employ a dual-channel model. After experiments, we found that using the combination of Mel-Frequency Cepstral Coefficients (MFCCs) and Bag-of-Audio-Words (BoAWs) feature set extracted using Open-Source Crossmodal Bag-of-Words (openXBOW)[1] [6] tool as the model's input obtained the best recall rate on the development dataset. In addition to deep learning methods, we also employed the traditional machine learning methods for classification, such as the Xgboost classifier using the ComParE Acoustic Feature Set (ComParE) manual features extracted by opensmile[2] [7]. The experimental results show that while Xgboost works well in most machine learning classification tasks, but using Xgboost alone results in lower recall for most labels than the CRNN. Instead of using the traditional voting method, we smooth the prediction sequences of the two models using the L2 norm to perform a model fusion. Data augmentation methods such as changing the speed and volume of the sound are used to enhance robustness. The main contribution of the paper can be summarized as below:

- We propose a Dual-channel Recurrent Neural Network with Xgboost to solve emotion recognition using nonspeech vocalizations.
- We employ a smoothing mechanism to integrate the two-channel neural network classifier and the xgboost classifier.
- We designed a transformer convolutional recurrent network as a substitute design to the traditional CRNN structure.

The rest of this article is organized as follows. In Sect. 2, related work is briefly described. In Sect. 3, we illustrate the proposed method in detail. In Sect. 4, the experimental results are presented. Conclusions and future work are provided in Sect. 5.

2   Related Works

In the past decade, the advancement of deep learning technologies has achieved increased accuracy of artificial intelligence speech emotion recognition. In Han's

---

[1] https://github.com/openXBOW/openXBOW
[2] http://github.com/audeering/opensmile

work [8], the Deep Neural Networks (DNNs) are used to extract effective emotional features from short-term low-level descriptors, which in turn fed into other classifiers for emotion recognition. Latif [9] proposed to use the most primitive time-frequency band speech data for convolution to complete the emotion recognition work. Compared with the most original band data as input, the mainstream method is to use various spectrograms combined with CRNN to complete the Speech Emotion Recognition (SER). By observing the spectrogram, we can better distinguish the phoneme attributes and formant attributes to better identify the sound. CRNN was first proposed by Baoguang and Xiang [10] to solve text classification tasks. Later on, researchers applied it to the emotion recognition tasks. It achieved good experimental results. Satt [5] and Sainath [11] proposed to use the spectrogram as input to capture the speech emotion information contained in the spectrogram. They use the convolutional neural network and Long short-term memory (LSTM) to perform a discrete emotion prediction and classification task. Coincidentally, this two studies [12, 13] performed good sentiment classification on the RECOLA database using an end-to-end model combining CNN and LSTM layers. People use different representations of features in the SER tasks. For example, in [14], two convolution kernels of different sizes are used to perform spatial convolution, and temporal convolution on input MFCCs features, while [15, 16] use manual feature sets for SER tasks. In addition, studies have shown that the introduction of transformer blocks [17] can effectively improve the performance of the model for multi-channel sentiment analysis and emotion recognition [18].

Overall, Researchers have been exploring various features and models to improve performance for SER tasks. Our solution to this problem is to combine hand-crafted features, i.e., deep learning and machine learning to achieve better model performance with ensemble learning.

3 Proposed Method

In this work, we combined the dual-channel neural network model and the XGBoost classifier as a base structure to explore the possibility of discovering emotional information from non-vocal speech. To benefit from the high concentration of MFCCs and the complementarity of xbow features, we use dual channels on DNN-based structures, CNN+LSTM based-structure, and Transformer based-structure. Then the two classification prediction sequences are integrated through the L2 norm, and it turns out that after smoothing, a more reasonable and effective final prediction result can be obtained, thereby achieving a higher UAR.

3.1 Dual-Channel Neural Network Model

We refer to the Luo's design [19] to establish the two Channel neural network model, and its overall framework is shown in Fig. 1. We put MFCCs and BoAWs manual features into two parallel channels. The CRNN channel uses MFCCs as input, while the DNN channel uses BoAWs as input. The outputs of each channel are mapped to the same feature space. It is then concatenated as the input to the fully connected layer. Finally, We use the Classification Block to perform the sentiment classification.

Figure 2 shows Channel 1's detailed design. We extract the speech signal into 40-dimensional MFCC features as the input to the first channel. We also tried 20-dimensional, 60-dimensional, and 80-dimensional MFCC features and found that feature size 40 works best. Then the convolution is performed through two convolutional layers. The size of the convolution kernel is 3×3. The number of feature maps in the first layer is 16, and the number of feature maps in the second layer is 32. After each convolutional layer is Batch Normalization and Relu activation unit, they enhance the generalization ability and expressive ability of the model. We use 2×2 max-pooling to downsample the feature map, therefore, reducing the dimension and the model size. It further reduces the risk of overfitting. The output of the previous layers is then processed by a 2-layer LSTM network. The LSTM network can solve the RNN's long-term dependency problem and has better performance in the time series prediction. Each LSTM network has 128 units. We use 0.5 as the dropout rate. The outputs of the LSTM's last time series for each layer are then concatenated. It is then fed to a fully connected layer to produce a 64-dimensional output.

The detailed design of channel 2 is shown in Fig. 3. We use the BoAWs feature set, which has 2000 feature dimensions. We also tried other feature sets offered by organizers, such as ComParE, DeepSpectrum, and auDeep. We found that none of them worked as well as BoAWs. The DNN model we use consists of three fully connected layers and produce a 64-dimensional output.

In the classification block, the outputs of the two channels are concatenated and classified into one of 6 emotion categories through a fully connected layer with softmax activation units.

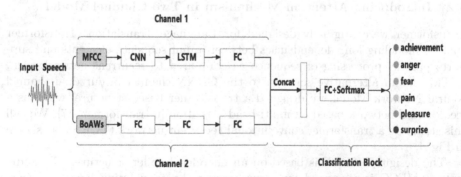

Fig. 1. Schematic diagram of proposed dual-model

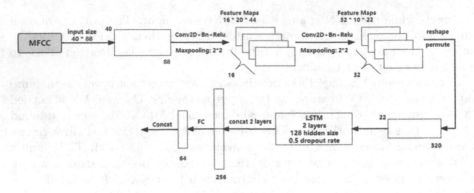

Fig. 2. Channel 1 detailed design

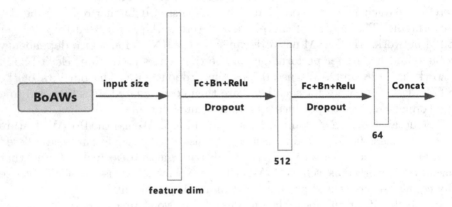

Fig. 3. Channel 2 detailed design

3.2 Introducing Attention Mechanism in Two-Channel Model

Transformer were originally designed for Language Translation. Transformer enables modeling long dependencies between input sequence elements and supports parallel processing of sequence as compared to recurrent networks e.g., LSTM. As an alternative solution to the CRNN channel in our dual-channel Neural Network Model, we designed a transformer based-structure, which is a feedforward network based on multi-head attention in transformer [17]. We call this structure a transformer convolutional recurrent network (TCRN), as shown in Fig. 4.

The design of TCRN is based on an encoder-decoder structure. The audio feature MFCC is processed by preprocessing the convolution layer and then sent to four encoder layers. The structure of the encoder is the same as the encoder layer in transformer [17]. In the Multi-head Attention block, we used four attention heads. The multi-head attention network maps a plurality of heads in different spaces to extract cross-location information.

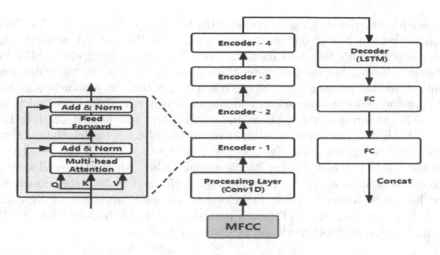

Fig. 4. Transformer convolution recurrent network

We use LSTM as our decoder in TCRN. LSTM is a neural network with a cyclic structure, which is composed of multiple network units (Cell). The parameters are shared among different network units. After receiving the input of the current time at time t, the network unit calculates the value of the hidden layer and then outputs the result of the current time. Unlike the network structure without timing, the hidden layer value not only depends on the input at the current moment but also is related to the hidden layer state at the previous moment. This connectivity property allows such networks to retain the memory of previous inputs, enabling them to process time series. The input gate, forget gate, and output gate is referenced in LSTM, which can effectively memorize information in a longer time dimension.

We use a two-layer LSTM for decoding, Each hidden layer has 128 units, and 0.5 is the dropout rate. Finally, input the decoding information of LSTM into two fully connected layers. It produces a 64-dimension output. Concatenated with the output from Channel 2, We have the final prediction with the Softmax function.

3.3   XGBoost Classifier

Since the dual-channel neural network model performance on some labels is not satisfying, our team considered various machine learning methods, specifically boosting methods.

XGBoost[3] is an open source software library, an implementation of the Xgboost algorithm, which provides a regularized gradient boosting framework. Through its optimization step, it is able to turn a large sum of weak learners into strong learners. Its regularization step helps prevent overfitting problems. It also

---

[b] https://github.com/dmlc/xgboost.

comes with a customized loss function. In the training process, we use ComParE Acoustic Feature Set as our input feature set since this dataset performs the best compared with the other datasets. Furthermore, we use gridsearchCV for parameter tuning. For the parameter tuning process, we use the entire development set and the training set as input. When we got the best parameters for the model, we used the training set for training and the development set to calculate the UAR. As a result, the UAR on the development set reached 42.01%. The overall UAR does not perform better than the two-channel model. However, we found from the results that Xgboost performs much better in the recall rate in some labels, especially in the "achievement" label, where the recall rate of Xgboost is as high as 44.4%. It is the best performance of all the models we used for the achievement label. Therefore, we do not simply discard Xgboost, instead, we take its result and smooth it together with the dual-channel model's result. The specific label recall will be displayed in Fig. 5.

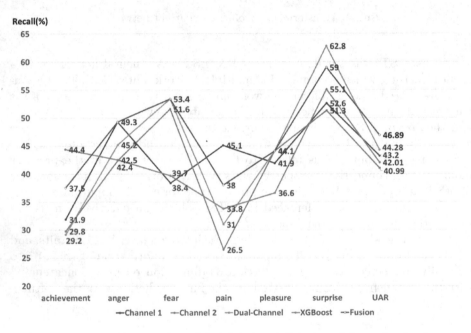

Fig. 5. Comparison of recall rate of each label in different models on the development set.

3.4   Model Fusion Using L2 Norm

Assuming

$$\boldsymbol{A_j} = (a_{j0}, a_{j1}, ..., a_{j5}) \tag{1}$$

is the prediction sequence of j sample of the two-channel model and

$$\boldsymbol{B_j} = (b_{j0}, b_{j1}, ...b_{j5}) \tag{2}$$

is the prediction sequence of j sample of the Xgboost model, we combine the array of corresponding positions into a two-dimensional vector,

$$C_{ji} = (a_{ji}, b_{ji}) \tag{3}$$

then calculate the L2 norm of this two-dimensional vector as the final predicted probability of the i_th label of the j_th sample

$$p_{ji} = \sqrt{a_{ji}^2 + b_{ji}^2}, i \in [0, 6] \tag{4}$$

4 Experiments

4.1 Datasets Used

We use Vocalisation Corpus VOC-C as our dataset, which is provided by Natalie Holz, MPI. Frankfurt is Main, features vocalizations (affect bursts) such as laughter, cries, moans, or screams, which have different affective intensities, and indicate different emotions [1]. The data set consists of 625 Train sets and 460 Development sets, of which are all female voices. The test set has 276 male voices. These data sets have 6 labels, including Achievement, Anger, Fear, Pain, Pleasure, and Surprise. The duration of each sample is about 1 s. The number of each type of label in this database is relatively balanced, so no compensation measures are needed.

4.2 Experimental Setup

In channel 1, we extract the MFCC features of the speech as the input to CRNN or TCRN model. First, we align the input speech data to a one-second length via truncation or zero-padding. We then call the librosa[4] library to generate 40×88 dimension MFCC features.

The input feature of channel 2 is the 2000 dimension BoAWs. We select DNN as the channel 2 standard model. Xgboost selects the entire data of the ComParE feature set as input.

For each training process, the two-channel model was trained for 80 epochs with a batch size 32. The cross-entropy criterion is used as the loss function. Using Adam as an optimizer, the weight decay rate is set to 2×10^{-5}. The initial learning rate is 10^{-3}, and its decay rate is 0.97. In the Xgboost experiment, we set the learning rate to 0.3, min-child-weight to 1, and max-depth to 6. We use the UAR metric to evaluate SER performance. UAR index can better deal with the uneven distribution of sample labels.

---

[4] https://github.com/librosa/librosa.

4.3   Experimental Results

In this experiment, channel 1 and channel 2 of the dual-channel Neural network model were optimized and predicted, respectively, and then the dual-channel joint prediction classification was carried out after they were adjusted to the optimal parameter configuration. The classification effect of each model is shown in Fig. 5.

Figure 5 shows UAR results of channel 1 and channel 2, which are 43.20% and 40.99%. The dual-channel Neural Network model has better results with UAR reaching 44.28%, indicating the model's effectiveness. XGBoost's classification effect is shown in the XGBoost branch in Fig. 5 and its overall UAR is 42.01%. After model fusion, its final UAR was 46.89%. All UAR results are shown in Table 1. The confusion matrix results of each emotion label are shown in Fig. 6.

From the above results, we can see that Channel 1 based on CRNN and Channel 2 based on full connection layer. They have already had good classification results. The convolutional layer in Channel 1 captures high-level abstraction, followed by the LSTM layer which performs the long-term temporal modelling. The fully connected layer in both channel performs discriminative representations which improve the classification results of the model. At the same time, the classificaiton block results are fused with the XGBoost classification results, and they complement each other, such achieve better final classification results.

Table 1. UAR results for each channel in Devel

Channel	UAR (%)
Channel 1	43.20
Channel 2	40.99
Dual-channel neural network model	44.28
XGBoost	42.01
Our result	**46.89**
Baseline	39.8

4.4   Introduce Attention Mechanism

In this experiment, we introduce the attention mechanism into the experiment of emotion classification and encode the input feature information through the stack of multi-head attention and feed-forward convolution. Experiments show that the introduction of the attention mechanism has a good improvement in emotion recognition. The model converges quickly during training, and only 9 epoch converges to the highest UAR: 0.44, as shown in Fig. 7. Where The horizontal axis is the training epoch, and the vertical axis is the UAR on the validation set. It can be seen that the model reaches convergence faster and maintains a good validation set UAR.

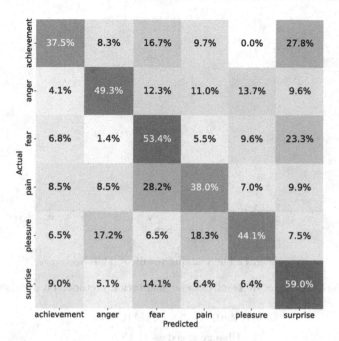

Fig. 6. Confusion Matrix of Fusion result on the development set.

We use TCRN to replace the Channel 1 CRNN in the two-channel model for feature learning of MFCC features. The experimental results show that our emotion recognition UAR results are similar to CRNN, but the convergence speed of the model during training and its stability performance, robustness, and generalization ability is further enhanced, which may be due to the attention mechanism, Dropout [20], and Batch Normalization [21] operations introduced in the network layers.

4.5   Data Augmentation

The dual-channel neural network model was used to evaluate the impacts of multiple data augmentation methods. All audio processing is done by calling the Libros library.

We changed the speed of sound and volume in the training dataset, the results are shown in Table 2. The two data enhancements did not bring an improvement in performance or even a decrease.

In the Vocalisation Corpus VOC-C, both the training and development sets have female vocalizations only, while the test set has male vocalizations only. Gender-specific differences in vocal annotation necessitate audio pitch transformation in the dataset. Male and female sound conversion is essential to ensure that the system has a better performance. Without the male-to-female voice conversion, the system only achieved a UAR of 46.89% on the training set and 30.4% on the test set.

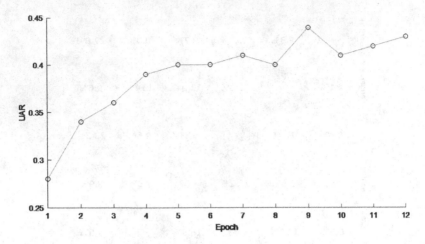

Fig. 7. The training result of TCRN

Table 2. Performance of different data augmentation methods on development set

Method	UAR
Change speed	44.15%
Change volume	44.02%
Raw data	44.28%

To achieve gender-specific sound transitions, we use Parselmouth[5], a python library for the Praat software, to achieve pitch shift without affecting factors such as speed of sound. In the conversion process, we tried two different conversions, i.e., male to female in the test set and female to male in the training and development sets. After evaluation, we found that converting the training and development sets to male voices worked better. It produced a final result of 37.0% UAR on the test set (Table 3).

Table 3. Performance of different speech gender conversion method

Method	UAR
Without Conversion	30.4%
Male to Female	36.3%
Female to Male	37.0%

---

[5] https://github.com/YannickJadoul/Parselmouth.

5   Conclusion

In this paper, we propose a dual-channel neural network model using CRNN and DNN and achieve a UAR 4% higher than the baseline on the development set. Moreover, we replace the CRNN with the TCRN model using the attention mechanism to improve the stability and robustness of the SER system. And We use Xgboost to work on the dataset and achieved a UAR 2% higher than the baseline on the development set. Then, we design a smoothing method to integrate the two widely used models, which consequently improves the UAR by 6%. Additionally, Data augmentation strategies are also discussed. In particular, the differences between male and female voices result in a considerable gap between performance on the test dataset and the development dataset. In future work, we will try to find a way to reduce the model's sensitivity to the characteristics caused by individual differences.

References

1. Schuller, B.W., et al.: The ACM multimedia 2022 computational paralinguistics challenge: vocalisations, stuttering, activity, & mosquitos. In: Proceedings ACM Multimedia 2022, Lisbon, Portugal, ISCA, October 2022 (to appear)
2. Yan, H., He, Q., Xie, W.: CRNN-CTC based mandarin keywords spotting. In: IEEE International Conference on Acoustics, Speech and Signal Processing (ICASSP), pp. 7489–7493 (2020)
3. Meftah, A.H., Mathkour, H., Kerrache, S., Alotaibi, Y.A.: Speaker identification in different emotional states in Arabic and English. IEEE Access 8, 60070–60083 (2020)
4. Ma, X., Wu, Z., Jia, J., Xu, M., Meng, H., Cai, L.: Emotion recognition from variable-length speech segments using deep learning on spectrograms. 09, 3683–3687 (2018)
5. Satt, A., Rozenberg, S., Hoory, R.: Efficient emotion recognition from speech using deep learning on spectrograms. 08, 1089–1093 (2017)
6. Schmitt, M., Schuller, B.: Openxbow - introducing the Passau open-source cross-modal bag-of-words toolkit. J. Mach. Learn. Res. 18, 1–5 (2017)
7. Eyben, F., Wöllmer, M., Schuller, B.: Opensmile - the Munich versatile and fast open-source audio feature extractor. 1459–1462 (2010)
8. Han, K., Yu, D., Tashev, I.: Speech emotion recognition using deep neural network and extreme learning machine (2014)
9. Latif, S., Rana, R., Khalifa, S., Jurdak, R., Epps, J.: Direct modelling of speech emotion from raw speech (2019)
10. Shi, B., Bai, X., Yao, C.: An end-to-end trainable neural network for image-based sequence recognition and its application to scene text recognition. IEEE Trans. Pattern Anal. Mach. Intell. 39(11), 2298–2304 (2017)
11. Sainath, T.N., Vinyals, O., Senior, A., Sak, H.: Convolutional, long short-term memory, fully connected deep neural networks. In: IEEE International Conference on Acoustics, Speech and Signal Processing (ICASSP), pp. 4580–4584 (2015)
12. Trigeorgis, G., Ringeval, F., Brueckner, R., Marchi, E., Zafeiriou, S.: Adieu features? End-to-end speech emotion recognition using a deep convolutional recurrent network. In: IEEE International Conference on Acoustics (2016)

13. Tzirakis, P., Zhang, J., Schuller, B.: End-to-end speech emotion recognition using deep neural networks. In: IEEE International Conference on Acoustics, Speech and Signal Processing (ICASSP) (2018)
14. Zhu, W., Li, X.: Speech emotion recognition with global-aware fusion on multi-scale feature representation (2022)
15. Kim, J., Saurous, R.A.: Emotion recognition from human speech using temporal information and deep learning. In: InterSpeech 2018 (2018)
16. Jian, H., Li, Y., Tao, J., Zheng, L.: Speech emotion recognition from variable-length inputs with triplet loss function. In: InterSpeech 2018 (2018)
17. Vaswani, A., et al.: Attention is all you need. arXiv (2017)
18. Zadeh, A., Liang, P.P., Poria, S., Vij, P., Cambria, E., Morency, L.P.: Multi-attention recurrent network for human communication comprehension. In: Proceedings of Conference on AAAI Artificial Intelligence, pp. 5642–5649 (2018)
19. Luo, D., Zou, Y., Huang, D.: Investigation on joint representation learning for robust feature extraction in speech emotion recognition. In: InterSpeech 2018 (2018)
20. Srivastava, N., Hinton, G., Krizhevsky, A., Sutskever, I., Salakhutdinov, R.: Dropout: a simple way to prevent neural networks from overfitting. J. Mach. Learn. Res. **15**(1), 1929–1958 (2014)
21. Ioffe, S., Szegedy, C.: Batch normalization: accelerating deep network training by reducing internal covariate shift. JMLR.org (2015)

STaR: Knowledge Graph Embedding by Scaling, Translation and Rotation

Jiayi Li and Yujiu Yang[✉]

Shenzhen International Graduate School, Tsinghua University, Beijing, China
lijy20@mails.tsinghua.edu.cn, yang.yujiu@sz.tsinghua.edu.cn

Abstract. The bilinear method is mainstream in Knowledge Graph Embedding (KGE), aiming to learn low-dimensional representations for entities and relations in Knowledge Graph (KG) and complete missing links. Most of the existing works are to find patterns between relationships and effectively model them to accomplish this task. Previous works have mainly discovered 6 important patterns like non-commutativity. Although some bilinear methods succeed in modeling these patterns, they neglect to handle 1-to-N, N-to-1, and N-to-N relations (or complex relations) concurrently, which hurts their expressiveness. To this end, we integrate scaling, the combination of translation and rotation that can solve complex relations and patterns, respectively, where scaling is a simplification of projection. Therefore, we propose a corresponding bilinear model Scaling Translation and Rotation (STaR) consisting of the above two parts. Besides, since translation can not be incorporated into the bilinear model directly, we introduce translation matrix as the equivalent. Theoretical analysis proves that STaR is capable of modeling all patterns and handling complex relations simultaneously, and experiments demonstrate its effectiveness on commonly used benchmarks for link prediction.

1 Introduction

Knowledge Graph (KG), storing data as triples like (head entity, relation, tail entity), is a growing way to deal with relational data. It has attracted the attention of researchers in recent years due to its applications in boosting other fields such as question answering [1], recommended systems [2], and natural language processing [3,4].

Since KG is usually incomplete, it needs to be completed by predicting the missing edges. A popular and effective way to accomplish this task is Knowledge Graph Embedding (KGE), which aims to find appropriate low-dimensional representations for entities and relations.

A mainstream of KGE is the bilinear method, which uses the product of entities and relations as a similarity. While two major problems in KGE are how to model different relation patterns and how to handle 1-to-N, N-to-1, and N-to-N relations (or complex relations) [5–7]. For the first problem, previous studies

---

Supplementary Information The online version contains supplementary material available at https://doi.org/10.1007/978-3-031-23504-7_3.

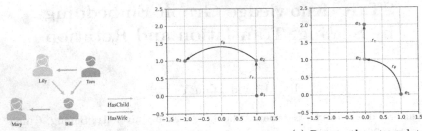

(a) Complex   relations (b) Translate then rotate. (c) Rotate then translate.
and   non-commutativity
pattern.

Fig. 1. Fig. 1(a) gives examples of N-to-1 relation and non-commutativity pattern. Figure 1(b) and Fig. 1(c) show how translation and rotation model non-commutativity patterns.

have mainly discovered 6 patterns [5,8,9]. For example, as shown in Fig. 1(a), *HasChild* and *HasWife* form a non-commutativity pattern, since the child of Tom's wife is Bill while the wife of Tom's child is Mary. For the second problem, we take an N-to-1 relation *HasChild* as an example illustrated in the same figure, in which Bill is the child of both Lily and Tom.

Although some recent works have successfully modeled different relation patterns, they neglect to handle complex relations concurrently. To be more specific, they represent relations as rotations (or reflections) to model different patterns like DihEdral [8] and QuatE [10], yet ignore that naive rotation is just like translation in TransE [11], which is difficult to handle complex relations.

To this end, we borrow the ideas from distance-based methods to go beyond rotation and solve these two problems simultaneously. Specifically, we combine projection that handles complex relations [6,7] and the combination of translation and rotation that models relation patterns [12], e.g. we demonstrate how they model non-commutativity in Fig. 1(b) and Fig. 1(c). Thus, we propose a corresponding bilinear model **S**caling **T**ranslation **a**nd **R**otation (STaR), where scaling is a simplification of projection and translation is introduced as matrix widely used in Robotics [13]. STaR can model different patterns and handle complex relations concurrently, and takes linear rather than quadratic parameters to embed a relation efficiently. Comparing to previous bilinear models, STaR is closest to ComplEx [14], which is equivalent to the combination of rotation and scaling and will be compared in Sect. 5 minutely.

Experiments on different settings demonstrate the effectiveness of our model against previous ones, while elaborated analysis against ComplEx shows the changes brought about by translation and verifies that our model improves from modeling the non-commutativity pattern. The main contributions of this paper are as follows:

1. We propose a bilinear model STaR that can efficiently model relation patterns and handle complex relations concurrently.

2. To the best of our knowledge, this is the first work introducing translation to the bilinear model, which brings new modules to it and connect with distance-based methods.
3. The proposed STaR achieves comparable results on three commonly used benchmarks for link prediction.

2   Related Work

Generally speaking, previous works on KGE can be divided into bilinear, distance-based, and other methods.

Bilinear Methods

Bilinear Methods measure the similarity of head and tail entities by their inner product under a relation specific transformation represented by a matrix R. RESCAL [15] is the ancestor of all bilinear models, whose R is arbitrary and has n^2 parameters. RESCAL is expressive yet ponderous and tends to overfit. To alleviate this issue, DistMult [16] uses diagonal matrices and reduces n^2 to n. ComplEx [14] transforms DistMult into complex spaces to model anti-symmetry pattern. Analogy [17] considers analogical pattern, which is equivalent to commutativity pattern, and generalizes DistMult, ComplEx, and HolE [18]. Although these descendants are powerful in handling complex relations and some patterns, they fail to model non-commutativity patterns.

The non-commutativity pattern was proposed by DihEdral [8] which uses a dihedral group to model all patterns. Besides, this pattern can also be modeled by hypercomplex values like quaternion or octonion used in QuatE [10]. Although they succeed in modeling non-commutativity, they are poor at handling complex relations. Thus, none of the previous bilinear methods has intended to handle relations and model concurrently.

Distance-Based Methods

In contrast, Distance-Based Methods use distance to measure the similarity. TransE [11] inspired by word2vec [19] proposes the first distance-based model and model relation as translation. TransH [6], TransR [7] find that TransE is incapable to model complex relations like *part_of* and fix this problem by projecting entities into relation-specific hyperspaces.

RotatE [5] utilizes rotation to model inversion and other patterns. Due to its success, subsequent models adopt the idea of rotation. HAKE [20] argues that rotation is incompetent to model hierarchical structures and introduces a radial part. MuRE [21] incorporates rotation with scaling while RotE [12] combines rotation and translation. Besides, they also have hyperbolic versions as MuRP and RotH. PairRE [22] also tries to model both the problems of patterns and complexity together, yet neglects the non-commutativity pattern.

Table 1. The score function and ability to model relation patterns of several models.

Model	Score function	Relation patterns						Performance on Complex Relations
		Composition	Symmetry	Anti-symmetry	Commutativity	Non-commutativity	Inversion	
TransE	$-\|h + r - t\|$	✓	✗	✓	✓	✗	✓	Low
TransR	$-\|M_r h + r - M_r t\|$	✓	✓	✓	✓	✓	✓	High
RotatE	$-\|h \circ r - t\|$	✓	✓	✓	✓	✗	✓	Low
MuRE	$-\|\rho \circ h + r - t\|$	✓	✓	✓	✓	✓	✓	Low
RotE	$-\|h Rot(\theta_r) + r - t\|$	✓	✓	✓	✓	✓	✓	Low
DistMult	$h^T \text{diag}(r)t$	✓	✓	✗	✓	✗	✓	High
ComplEx	$\text{RE}(h^T \text{diag}(r)\bar{t})$	✓	✓	✓	✓	✗	✓	High
QuatE	$Q_h \otimes W_r^\triangleleft \cdot Q_t$	✓	✓	✓	✓	✓	✓	Low
STaR	$\hat{h}^T R_r \hat{t}$	✓	✓	✓	✓	✓	✓	High

Other Methods

Apart from the above two, some studies also employ black boxes or external information. ConvE [23] and ConKB [24] utilize convolution neural network while R-GCN [25] and RGHAT [26] apply graph neural networks. Besides, some other works use external information like text [27,28], while they are out of our consideration.

Besides specific models, other researchers believe that some previous models are limited by overfitting. Thus, they propose better regularization terms like N3 [29] and DURA [30] to handle this problem.

3   Methodology

In this section, we will first introduce the background knowledge. Then, we will propose our model STaR by combining the useful modules that solve patterns and complex relations. Finally, we will discuss the translation in the bilinear model.

3.1   Background Knowledge

Knowledge Graph. Given an entity set $\mathcal{E}$ and a relation set $\mathcal{R}$, A knowledge graph $\mathcal{T} = (h_i, r_j, t_k) \subset \mathcal{E} \times \mathcal{R} \times \mathcal{E}$ is a set of triples, where h_i, r_j, t_k, denotes the head entity, relation and tail entity respectively. The number of entities and relations are indicated by $|\mathcal{E}|$ and $|\mathcal{R}|$.

Problem Definition. Knowledge graph embedding aims to learn a score function $s(h, r, t)$ and the embeddings of entities and relations, which uses the link prediction task to evaluate the performance. Link prediction first splits triples of the knowledge graph $\mathcal{T}$ into train set $\mathcal{T}_{train}$, test set $\mathcal{T}_{test}$ and valid set $\mathcal{T}_{valid}$. Then, for each specific triple in $\mathcal{T}_{test}$, link prediction aims to give the correct entity $tail \in \mathcal{E}$ a lower rank than other candidates given the query $(head, relation, ?)$ or head entity $head \in \mathcal{E}$ given the query $(?, relation, tail)$ by utilizing the score function.

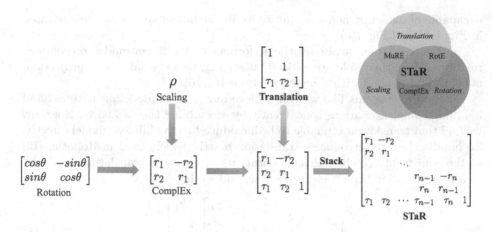

Fig. 2. How STaR consists of 3 basic operations and model and related to 3 previous models.

Complex Relations. The complex relations are defined by tails per head and heads per tail of a relation r (tphr and hptr) [6]. If tphr > 1.5 and hptr < 1.5 then r is 1-to-N while tphr > 1.5 and hptr > 1.5 means r corresponds to N-to-N.

Relation Patterns. Relation patterns are the inherent semantic characteristics of relations, which are helpful to model relations and inference.

Previous works have mainly proposed 6 patterns [8,9]. They are **Composition** (e.g., my father's brother is my uncle), **Symmetry** (e.g., *IsSimilarTo*), **Anti-Symmetry** (e.g., *IsFatherOf*), **Commutativity**, **Non-Commutativity** (e.g., *my wife's son is not my son's wife*), **Inversion**. For the formal definition of all patterns, please refer to Supplementary Material A.

Other Notations. We use $h \in \mathbb{R}^{n \times 1}$ and $t \in \mathbb{R}^{n \times 1}$ to denote the embedding of head entity and tail entity respectively, where n is the embedding dimension. And we use $\circ$ to denote the relation composition. For example, if we take $r_1, r_2, r_3 \in \mathcal{R}$, and r_3 is the composition of r_1 and r_2 then $r_3 = r_1 \circ r_2$.

3.2 The Proposed STaR Model

In this part, we will analyze modules in previous works that model different patterns and handle complex relations. Then we will propose a bilinear model Scaling Translation and Rotation (**STaR**).

In Table 1, we list the score function $s(h, r, t)$ of different models and their ability to model patterns, where we observe that the stickiest one is non-commutativity. To model it, QuatE [10] utilizes quaternion to model the rotation in 3D space. However, we think it is unnecessary to introduce hypercomplex values and redefine the product operator. In contrast, we are inspired by a distance-based model RotE [12] that uses the combination of translation and rotation and is capable of modeling non-commutativity in Euclidean spaces as demonstrated in Fig. 1(b) and Fig. 1(c).

In the same table, we also list the performance of different models on complex relations. From this table, we notice that scaling, as a special case of projection, is helpful for dealing with complex relations [14, 16].

Therefore, it seems like we can achieve our goal of modeling patterns and handling complex relations concurrently by assembling the two parts. However, we find that translation is unable to be introduced to the bilinear model directly. To handle this, we introduce a translation matrix widely used in Robotics [13] as the equivalent. To show this substitution, we choose a translation $\tau \in \mathbb{R}^{1 \times n}$ to a point $x \in \mathbb{R}^{1 \times n}$ in $\mathbb{R}^n$ as an example, and we have:

$$
\begin{bmatrix} x \\ 1 \end{bmatrix} + \begin{bmatrix} \tau \\ 1 \end{bmatrix} = \begin{bmatrix} 1 & & \tau_1 \\ & \ddots & \vdots \\ & 1 & \tau_n \\ & & 1 \end{bmatrix} \begin{bmatrix} x_1 \\ \vdots \\ x_n \\ 1 \end{bmatrix}, \tag{1}
$$

where the matrix is the translation matrix.

Finally, we achieve the proposed **S**caling **T**anslation **a**nd **R**otation (**STaR**) model by combing such three modules and stacking these elementary blocks as demonstrated in Fig. 2, where ComplEx can be treated as the combination of rotation and scaling in two dimensions manner.

The representation of a relation is thus achieved by assembling a ComplEx matrix with a translation offset:

$$
R_* = \begin{bmatrix} R_c \\ \tau^T & 1 \end{bmatrix}, \tag{2}
$$

where $R_c \in \mathbb{R}^{n \times n}$ and $\tau \in \mathbb{R}^{n \times 1}$ denotes the relation specific ComplEx matrix and translation offset respectively. Besides R_c is achieved by a vector $r^c \in \mathbb{R}^{n \times 1}$ as:

$$
R_c = \begin{bmatrix} r_1^c & -r_2^c & & & \\ r_2^c & r_1^c & & & \\ & & \ddots & & \\ & & & r_{n-1}^c & -r_n^c \\ & & & r_n^c & r_{n-1}^c \end{bmatrix}. \tag{3}
$$

Therefore, the score function of STaR is:

$$
s(h, r, t) = \hat{h}^T R_* \hat{t}, \tag{4}
$$

where $\hat{h} = [h^T, 1]^T$ and $\hat{t} = [t^T, 1]^T$.

From the score function, STaR is proved to model all 6 patterns and handle complex relations as detailed in Supplementary Material B.

Proposition 1. *STaR can model Symmetry, Anti-Symmetry, Composition, Inversion, Commutativity, and Non-Commutativity and handle complex relations concurrently.*

3.3   Discussions

In this part, we will detail what does translation brings to bilinear model and how it helps to model the non-commutativity minutely.

What Does Translation Bring to Bilinear Model? We unfold the score function of STaR in Eq. (4):

$$
\begin{aligned}
s(h, r, t) &= \hat{h}^T R_* \hat{t} \\
&= (h^T R_c + \tau^T) t + 1 \\
&= \underbrace{h^T R_c t}_{\text{ComplEx}} + \underbrace{\tau^T t}_{\text{E}} + 1.
\end{aligned}
\tag{5}
$$

Except the constant 1 comes from the extra dimension, the above equation shows that it has two parts: ComplEx and the model E proposed by [31]. The later part E is the dot product of the relation-specific translation τ and the candidate tail entity t regardless of the head entity. Therefore, E works like determining whether the tail entity suits the relation. For example, given a relation *IsLocatedIn*, it is impossible to be a correct triple with a tail entity like *Bill* or *Mary* no matter what the head entity is.

How Does Translation Help Model Non-commutativity? We take two relations $r_1, r_2 \in \mathcal{R}$, whose composited relation $r_3 = r_1 \circ r_2$ is represented as $R_*^1 \cdot R_*^2$. Similarly, we unfold the score function of a triple regarding r_3 as:

$$
\begin{aligned}
s(h, r_3, t) &= \hat{h}^T R_*^1 \cdot R_*^2 \hat{t} \\
&= \left((h^T R_c^1 + (\tau^1)^T) \cdot R_c^2 + (\tau^2)^T \right) t + 1 \\
&= \underbrace{h^T (R_c^1 R_c^2) t}_{\text{ComplEx}} + \underbrace{\left((\tau^1)^T R_c^2 + (\tau^2)^T \right) t}_{\text{E}} + 1.
\end{aligned}
\tag{6}
$$

The E in Eq. (5) reappears in Eq. (6). As shown in the Table 1, it is E, *per se*, helps ComplEx to model the non-commutativity pattern since $(\tau^1)^T R_c^2 + (\tau^2)^T \neq (\tau^2)^T R_c^1 + (\tau^1)^T$.

To better understand the role of E, we take r_1 as *IsWifeOf* and r_2 as *IsFatherOf* as an example. Then the wife of someone's father must be a woman, while the father of someone's wife must be a man, where the order of relations affects which tail entities are fitted.

4   Experiments

In this section, we will introduce the experiment settings and three benchmark datasets and show the comparable results of our model.

Table 2. Link prediction results on different benchmarks (best for $n \in \{200, 400, 500\}$. † means the results are taken from [12]. Since original paper of DURA [30] conduct on extremely high dimension, here we reimplement ComlEx-DURA and RESCAL-DURA. Best results are in **bold** while the seconds are underlined. STaR is our full model while TaR excludes scaling.

Model	WN18RR				FB15K237				YAGO3-10			
	MRR	Hits@1	Hits@3	Hits@10	MRR	Hits@1	Hits@3	Hits@10	MRR	Hits@1	Hits@3	Hits@10
DistMult†	0.43	0.39	0.44	0.49	0.241	0.155	0.263	0.419	0.34	0.24	0.38	0.54
ConvE†	0.43	0.40	0.44	0.52	0.325	0.237	0.356	0.501	0.44	0.35	0.49	0.62
TuckER†	0.470	0.443	0.482	0.526	0.358	0.266	0.394	0.544	–	–	–	–
QuatE†	0.488	0.438	0.508	0.582	0.348	0.248	0.382	0.550	–	–	–	–
RotatE†	0.476	0.428	0.492	0.571	0.338	0.241	0.375	0.533	0.495	0.402	0.550	0.670
MurP†	0.481	0.440	0.495	0.566	0.335	0.243	0.367	0.518	0.354	0.249	0.400	0.567
RotE†	0.494	0.446	<u>0.512</u>	<u>0.585</u>	0.346	0.251	0.381	0.538	0.574	0.498	<u>0.621</u>	<u>0.711</u>
RotH†	<u>0.496</u>	<u>0.449</u>	**0.514**	**0.586**	0.344	0.246	0.380	0.535	0.570	0.495	0.612	0.706
ComplEx-N3†	0.480	0.435	0.495	0.572	0.357	0.264	0.392	0.547	0.569	0.498	0.609	0.701
ComplEx-Fro	0.457	0.427	0.469	0.515	0.323	0.235	0.354	0.497	0.568	0.493	0.613	0.699
TaR-Fro (ours)	0.470	0.438	0.481	0.532	0.325	0.239	0.356	0.501	0.567	0.494	0.610	0.699
STaR-Fro (ours)	0.463	0.431	0.476	0.526	0.324	0.236	0.356	0.501	0.574	0.502	0.617	0.701
RESCAL-DURA	<u>0.496</u>	**0.452**	**0.514**	0.575	**0.370**	**0.278**	**0.406**	<u>0.553</u>	0.577	0.501	<u>0.621</u>	<u>0.711</u>
ComplEx-DURA	0.488	0.446	0.504	0.571	0.365	0.270	0.401	0.552	<u>0.578</u>	<u>0.507</u>	0.620	0.704
TaR-DURA (ours)	0.488	0.446	0.503	0.567	0.351	0.257	0.387	0.539	<u>0.578</u>	0.506	<u>0.621</u>	0.707
STaR-DURA (ours)	**0.497**	**0.452**	<u>0.512</u>	<u>0.583</u>	<u>0.368</u>	<u>0.273</u>	<u>0.405</u>	**0.557**	**0.585**	**0.513**	**0.628**	**0.713**

Table 3. Statistics of three benchmark datasets.

	WN18RR	FB15K237	YAGO3-10
$|\mathcal{E}|$	40,943	14,541	123,182
$|\mathcal{R}|$	11	237	37
Train	86,835	272,115	1,079,040
Valid	3,034	17,535	5,000
Test	3,134	20,466	5,000
Ψ	0.003	0.801	0.838

4.1   Experiments Settings

Datasets. We evaluate all models on the three most commonly used datasets, which are WN18RR [23], FB15K237 [31] and YAGO3-10 [32]. WN18RR and FB15K237 are the subsets of WordnNet and Freebase, respectively. They are the more challenging version of the previous WN18 and FB15K that suffer from data leakage [23,31]. We demonstrate the statistics of these benchmarks in Table 3. In particular, we use Ψ to denote the imbalance ratio of the train set, which will be introduced in Sect. 5.1

Baselines. We compare our method with previous models, which are Dist-Mult [16], ConvE [23], Tucker [33], QuatE [10], MurP [21], RotE and RotH [12] and some previous bilinear models with N3 [29] and DURA [30] regularization terms. Besides, we also propose TaR consisting of **T**ranslation and **R**otation for comparison.

Evaluation Metrics. We use the score functions to rank the correct tail (head) among all possible candidate entities. Following previous works, we use mean reciprocal rank (MRR) and Hits@K as evaluation metrics. MRR is the mean of the reciprocal rank of valid entities, avoiding the problem of mean rank (MR) being sensitive to outliers. Hits@K ($K \in \{1, 3, 10\}$ measures the proportion of proper entities ranked within the top K. Besides, we follow the filtered setting [11] which ignores those also correct candidates in ranking.

Optimization. Following [29], we use the cross-entropy loss and the reciprocal setting that adds a reciprocal relation $\tilde{r}$ for each relation $r \in \mathcal{R}$ and $(t, \tilde{r}, h)$ for each triple $(h, r, t) \in \mathcal{T}$:

$$\mathcal{L} = - \sum_{(h,r,t) \in \mathcal{T}_{train}} (\frac{\exp(s(h, r, t))}{\sum_{t' \in \mathcal{E}} \exp(s(h, r, t'))} w(t)$$
$$+ \frac{\exp(s(t, \tilde{r}, h))}{\sum_{h' \in \mathcal{E}} \exp(s(t, \tilde{r}, h'))} w(h)) \qquad (7)$$
$$+ \lambda \mathrm{Reg}(h, r, t),$$

where $\mathrm{Reg}(h, r, t)$ denotes the regularization and $w(t)(w(h))$ is the weight for the tail (head) entity:

$$w(t) = w_0 \frac{\#t}{max\{\#t_i : t_i \in \mathcal{T}_{train}\}} + (1 - w_0), \qquad (8)$$

where w_0 is a constant for each dataset, $\#t$ represents the count of entity t in the training set [30].

Besides, we use both Frobenius (Fro) and DURA [30] regularization for better comparison. For the details of DURA for STaR please refer to Supplementary Material C.

Implementation Details. We search the best results in $n \in \{200, 400, 500\}$. After searching for hyperparameters, we set the dimension to 500, the learning rate to 0.1 for all datasets, and the batch size to 100 for WN18RR and FB15K237 while 1000 for YAGO3-10. Besides, we choose $w_0 = 0.1$ for WN18RR and 0 for the others. Moreover, for DURA we use $\lambda = 0.1, 0.05, 0.005$ for WN18RR, FB15K237 and YAGO3-10 respectively, while for Frobinues (Fro) we use $\lambda = 0.001$ for all cases. Each result is an average of 5 runs.

4.2 Main Results

As shown in Table 2, STaR achieves comparable results against previous bilinear models. STaR improves more on WN18RR and YAGO3-10 than ComplEx under either Fro or DURA regularization. Moreover, STaR achieves similar results compared to RESCAL under DURA. Yet, STaR only needs $2n$ parameters to model

Table 4. The MRR of STaR-DURA and TaR-DURA on complex relations in WN18RR. Better results are in **bold**.

	1-to-1	1-to-N	N-to-1	N-to-N
TaR-DURA	**0.965**	0.248	0.206	0.943
STaR-DURA	0.922	**0.260**	**0.226**	0.943

a relation while RESCAL requires n^2, which shows the efficiency of our model. Besides, STaR still improves about 1% on YAGO3-10 compared to RESCAL.

Comparing with the distance-based baselines RotE and RotH [12], STaR outperforms them on FB15K237 and YAGO3-10 significantly and gets similar results on WN18RR. Therefore, STaR is more versatile than those distance-based models, which owes scaling.

Besides, we observe that both translation and scaling require appropriate regularization to show their real effects. On the one hand, comparing with STaR-Fro, TaR-Fro achieves similar or even better results, which seems like scaling is useless. On the other hand, comparing with QuatE, TaR-Fro drops 2 point in WN18RR and FB15K237, which seems like translation and rotation in 2Ds are less powerful than rotation in 3Ds in QuatE. However, that is not the whole story. When we turn to a more powerful regularization term DURA, on the one hand, TaR-DURA is outperformed by STaR-DURA consistently since scaling helps to handle complex relations as shown in Table 4. On the other hand, TaR-DURA achieves similar results compared to QuatE as they both model all patterns yet are weak on complex relations. We think this phenomenon is because both scaling and translation lack the inborn normalization like rotation and thus require an appropriate regularization term to prevent overfitting.

5 Analysis

In this section, we will further compare STaR with ComplEx. Then we will analyze the benchmark KGs in a new perspective to explain the unexpected phenomenon in the comparison. Finally, we will verify that the improvement comes from modeling non-commutativity.

5.1 Further Comparison with ComplEx

To show STaR outperforms ComplEx consistently, we conduct further experiments in different dimensions and regularization terms. As shown in Fig. 3, STaR exceeds ComplEx on WN18RR persistently. Besides, both STaR and ComplEx improve by substituting DURA for Frobenius as the dimension increases. Additionally, STaR and ComplEx seem to intersect in an extremely high dimension, which leads us to further experiment in the following content.

As shown in the Table 5, STaR outperforms ComplEx on WN18RR prominently. However, these two are tied on FB15K237 and YAGO3-10 unexpectedly.

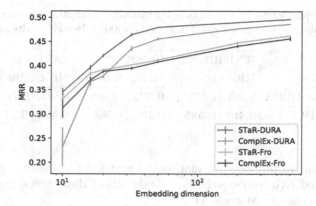

Fig. 3. Comparison of STaR and ComplEx on WN18RR under different dimensions ($n \in \{10, 16, 20, 32, 50, 200, 500\}$) and regularization terms (Fro and DURA). Averages and standard deviations are computed over 5 runs for each case.

We think such a phenomenon is due to the lack of non-commutativity patterns in them substantially. To verify our hypothesis, we further investigate those KGs from a new perspective.

5.2 Imbalance Ratio Among KGs

In this part, we will verify the above hypothesis by introducing two matrices ψ and Ψ about the imbalance ratio.

We find that modeling commutativity and non-commutativity is useful only if both possible orders of a pair of relations appear in a KG. For instance, consider two relations $r_1, r_2 \in \mathcal{R}$, which have two possible orders of composition: $r_1 \circ r_2$ and $r_2 \circ r_1$. Therefore, if only one of them, e.g., $r_1 \circ r_2$, exists in the KG, it is unnecessary to distinguish whether they are commutative or not.

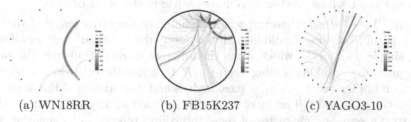

| (a) WN18RR | (b) FB15K237 | (c) YAGO3-10 |

Fig. 4. The count and imbalance ratio of all possible pairs. An arc represents a pair. On the one hand, pair imbalance ratio ψ is denoted by color, as blue means balance while gray means imbalance in contrast. On the other hand, the count is denoted by transparency and thickness, as thick and opaque means more while thin and transparent means less. It should be noticed that the thickness of the arcs is relative, so the arcs with the same thickness in different datasets may have different counts. (Color figure online)

Table 5. Link prediction results between STaR and ComplEx for extremely high-dimensional embedding (best for $n \in \{1000, 2000, 4000\}$). Better results are in **bold**.

Model	WN18RR		FB15K237		YAGO3-10	
	MRR	Hits@10	MRR	Hits@10	MRR	Hits@10
ComlEx-DURA	0.490	0.573	**0.371**	**0.561**	0.583	0.710
STaR-DURA	**0.499**	**0.585**	0.370	0.558	**0.584**	**0.713**

To this end, we propose two matrices ψ and Ψ to evaluate the imbalance ratio of pair and KG, respectively. For the details of these two matrices, please refer to Supplementary Material D.

Based on Ψ of each benchmark as shown in Table 3, we observe that the imbalance is remarkable in FK15K237 and YAGO3-10. Moreover, we are aware that although some pairs have both orders, the counts between orders may have an enormous discrepancy. To show this more specifically, we visualize the pairs of three benchmark KGs. As shown in Fig. 4, on the one hand, the majority of pairs are imbalanced in FB15K237 and YAGO3-10. On the other hand, although many imbalanced pairs exist in WN18RR, the balanced ones account for the majority as denoted by Ψ.

We believe the above analysis validates the hypothesis and explains the phenomenon. Furthermore, we think the discrepancy between KGs is rooted in the entities. Specifically, we notice that all entities are homogeneous in WordNet, which consists of words, while heterogeneous in Freebase and YAGO, built by various things like person, film, etc. Therefore, in KGs like WordNet, all relations connect things of the same kind. In contrast, in ones like Freebase and YAGO, most relations connect things of different kinds.

Therefore, for the relations in the imbalance KGs like FB15K237 and YAGO3-10, some pairs of them only have one meaningful order in the sense of semantics substantially. For instance, consider two relations: $isDirectedBy$ and $likeEating$, whose combination makes sense in the order of $film \xrightarrow{IsDirectedBy}$ $human \xrightarrow{likeEating} food$. However, when exchanging the order, we find that the tail entity of $likeEating$ should be a kind of food, and the head entity of $isDirectedBy$ should be a movie, which shows the inherent incompatibility in this order. More generally speaking, taking $\forall r_1, r_2 \in \mathcal{R}$ that has the order of combination $r_1 \circ r_2$. Its other order $r_2 \circ r_1$ is meaningless and nonexistent if the domain of head entity of r_1 and tail entity of r_2 are not intersected. In conclusion, we think that such a semantic character of these inter-kind relations explains the cause of the scarcity of non-commutativity in FB15K237 and YAGO3-10.

5.3 Improvements on WN18RR Come from Modeling Non-commutativity Pattern

In FB15K237 and YAGO3-10, we have shown that imbalances are prevalent and thus explain why STaR and ComplEx are tied. Here we further experiment to

Table 6. Comparison of the MRR of STaR and ComplEx on WN18RR. $\triangle$ denotes improvement and $\triangledown$ decreases on extremely high-dimensional settings.

Relation name	Propotion	STaR	ComplEx	Improvement
Hypernym	40.09%	0.193	0.175	10.29% $\triangle$
Derivationally related form	34.23%	0.956	0.959	−0.31% $\triangledown$
Member meronym	8.52%	0.241	0.225	7.11% $\triangle$
Has part	5.55%	0.247	0.230	7.39% $\triangle$
Synset domain topic of	3.56%	0.409	0.387	5.68% $\triangle$
Instance hypernym	3.37%	0.420	0.409	2.69% $\triangle$
Also see	1.49%	0.634	0.631	0.47% $\triangle$
Verb group	1.30%	0.917	0.975	−5.95% $\triangledown$
Member of domain region	1.06%	0.408	0.279	46.24% $\triangle$
Member of domain usage	0.73%	0.359	0.316	13.61% $\triangle$
Similar to	0.09%	1.000	1.000	0.00%

corroborate that the improvement on WN18RR gains from modeling the non-commutativity pattern.

As shown in Table 6, STaR surpasses ComplEx in most relations. Although STaR slightly decreases in *derivationally related form* which is already high enough, it gains about 10% in *hypernym* with the largest proportion. Correspondingly, we notice that in Fig. 4(a) the outstanding thick blue arc denotes both $e_1 \xrightarrow{hyp.} e_2 \xrightarrow{d.r.f.} e_3$ and $e_1 \xrightarrow{d.f.r.} e_2 \xrightarrow{hyp.} e_3$ are abundant in WN18RR[1]. Besides, we find that these two relations are non-commutative. Therefore, we think such a correspondence validates that the improvement on WN18RR comes from modeling non-commutativity.

6   Conclusion

In this paper, we notice that none of the previous bilinear models can model all patterns and handle complex relations simultaneously. To fill the gap, we propose a bilinear model **S**caling **T**ranslation **a**nd **R**otation (STaR) consisting of these three basic modules. STaR solves both problems concurrently and achieves comparable results compared to previous baselines. Moreover, we also conduct a deep investigation to verify that our model is improved by handling relations or modeling patterns that previous bilinear models failed.

Acknowledgment. This work was partially supported by the Shenzhen Key Laboratory of Marine IntelliSense and Computation under Grant No. ZDSYS2020081 1142605016 and AMiner · Science and Technology Superbrain Funding.

---

[1] *hyp.* and *d.f.r* stands for *hypernym* and *derivationally related form* respectively.

References

1. Mohammed, S., Shi, P., Lin, J.: Strong baselines for simple question answering over knowledge graphs with and without neural networks. In: NAACL-HLT (2), pp. 291–296 (2012)
2. Zhang, F., Yuan, N.J., Lian, D., Xie, X., Ma, W.: Collaborative knowledge base embedding for recommender systems. In: KDD, pp. 353–362 (2016)
3. Wang, J., Wang, Z., Zhang, D., Yan, J.: Combining knowledge with deep convolutional neural networks for short text classification. In: IJCAI, pp. 2915–2921 (2017)
4. Ji, S., Pan, S., Cambria, E., Marttinen, P., Yu, P.S.: A survey on knowledge graphs: representation, acquisition, and applications. IEEE Trans. Neural Netw. Learn Syst. **33**, 1–21 (2021)
5. Sun, Z., Deng, Z., Nie, J., Tang, J.: Rotate: Knowledge graph embedding by relational rotation in complex space. In: ICLR (2019)
6. Wang, Z., Zhang, J., Feng, J., Chen, Z.: Knowledge graph embedding by translating on hyperplanes. In: AAAI, pp. 1112–1119 (2014)
7. Lin, Y., Liu, Z., Sun, M., Liu, Y., Zhu, X.: Learning entity and relation embeddings for knowledge graph completion. In: AAAI, pp. 2181–2187 (2015)
8. Xu, C., Li, R.: Relation embedding with dihedral group in knowledge graph. In: ACL, pp. 263–272 (2019)
9. Yang, T., Sha, L., Hong, P.: NAGE: non-abelian group embedding for knowledge graphs. In: CIKM, pp. 1735–1742 (2020)
10. Zhang, S., Tay, Y., Yao, L., Liu, Q.: Quaternion knowledge graph embeddings. In: NeurIPS, pp. 2731–2741 (2019)
11. Bordes, A., et al.: Translating embeddings for modeling multi-relational data. In: NeurIPS, pp. 2787–2795 (2013)
12. Chami, I., Wolf, A., Juan, D., Sala, F., Ravi, S., Ré, C/.: Low-dimensional hyperbolic knowledge graph embeddings. In: ACL, pp. 6901–6914 (2020)
13. Paul, R.P.: Robot Manipulators: Mathematics, Programming, and Control: The Computer Control of Robot Manipulators. Richard Paul (1981)
14. Trouillon, T., Welbl, J., Riedel, S., Gaussier, aÉ., Bouchard, G.: Complex embeddings for simple link prediction. In: ICML, vol. 48, pp. 2071–2080 (2016)
15. Nickel, M., Tresp, V., Kriegel, H.: A three-way model for collective learning on multi-relational data. In: ICML, pp. 809–816 (2011)
16. Yang, B., Yih, W., He, X., Gao, J., Deng, L.: Embedding entities and relations for learning and inference in knowledge bases. In: ICLR (2015)
17. Liu, H., Wu, Y., Yang, Y.: Analogical inference for multi-relational embeddings. In: ICML, vol. 70, pp. 2168–2178 (2017)
18. Nickel, A., Rosasco, L., Poggio, T.A.: Holographic embeddings of knowledge graphs. In: AAAI, pp. 1955–1961 (2016)
19. Mikolov, T., Sutskever, I., Chen, K., Corrado, G.S., Dean, J.: Distributed representations of words and phrases and their compositionality. In: NeurIPS, pp. 3111–3119 (2013)
20. Zhang, Z., Cai, J., Zhang, Y., Wang, J.: Learning hierarchy-aware knowledge graph embeddings for link prediction. In: AAAI, pp. 3065–3072 (2020)
21. Balazevic, I., Allen, C., Hospedales, T.M.: Multi-relational poincaré graph embeddings. In: NeurIPS, pp. 4465–4475 (2019)
22. Chao, L., He, J., Wang, T., Chu, W.: Pairre: Knowledge graph embeddings via paired relation vectors. In: Zong, C., Xia, F., Li, W., Navigli, R. (eds.) ACL/IJCNLP, vol. 1, pp. 4360–4369 (2021)

23. Dettmers, T., Minervini, P., Stenetorp, P., Riedel, S.: Convolutional 2D knowledge graph embeddings. In: AAAI, pp. 1811–1818 (2018)
24. Nguyen, D.Q., Nguyen, T.D., Nguyen, Q., Phung, D.Q.: A novel embedding model for knowledge base completion based on convolutional neural network. In: NAACL-HLT, Issue 2, pp. 327–333 (2018)
25. Schlichtkrull, M.S., Kipf, T.N., Bloem, P., van den Berg, R., Titov, I., Welling, M.: Modeling relational data with graph convolutional networks. In: ESWC, vol. 10843, pp. 593–607 (2018)
26. Schlichtkrull, M.S., Kipf, T.N., Bloem, P., van den Berg, R., Titov, T., Welling, M.: Modeling relational data with graph convolutional networks. In: ESWC, vol. 10843, pp. 593–607 (2018)
27. An, B., Chen, B., Han, X., Sun, L.: Accurate text-enhanced knowledge graph representation learning. In: NAACL-HLT, pp. 745–755 (2018)
28. Yao, L., Mao, C., Luo, Y.: KG-BERT: BERT for knowledge graph completion (2019)
29. Lacroix, T., Usunier, N., Obozinski, G.: Canonical tensor decomposition for knowledge base completion. In: ICML, vol. 80, pp. 2869–2878 (2018)
30. Zhang, Z., Cai, J., Wang, J.: Duality-induced regularizer for tensor factorization based knowledge graph completion. In: NeurIPS (2020)
31. Toutanova, K., Chen, D.: Observed versus latent features for knowledge base and text inference. In: Proceedings of the 3rd Workshop on Continuous Vector Space Models and their Compositionality, Beijing, China, July 2015, pp. 57–66 (2015)
32. Mahdisoltani, F., Biega, J., Suchanek, F.M.: YAGO3: a knowledge base from multilingual wikipedias. In: CIDR (2015)
33. Balazevic, L., Allen, C., Hospedales, T.M.: Tucker: tensor factorization for knowledge graph completion. In: EMNLP/IJCNLP, pp. 5184–5193 (2019)

Application Track

Frequently Asked Question Pair Generation for Rule and Regulation Document

Keyang Ding[1,3], Chenran Cai[1,3], Shijue Huang[1,3], Rui Wang[1,3],
Qianlong Wang[1,3], Jianxin Li[2,3], Guozhong Shi[2,3], Feiran Hu[2,3], Fengxin Li[2,3],
and Ruifeng Xu[1,3(✉)]

[1] School of Computer Science and Technology,
Harbin Institute of Technology (Shenzhen), Shenzhen, China
{keyang.ding,22s151167,22s051040}@stu.hit.edu.cn, qlwang15@outlook.com,
xuruifeng@hit.edu.cn
[2] China Merchants Securities Co., Ltd., Shenzhen, China
[3] Joint Lab of HITSZ and China Merchants Securities, Shenzhen, China
{lijx,shiguozhong,hufeiran,lifengxin}@cmschina.com.cn

Abstract. This paper presents a novel task to generate frequently asked question (FAQ) pairs for the rule and regulation documents. It offers an easy way for customers and employers to quickly gain knowledge of them and provides a potential corpus for question-answering robots. While previous work focuses on web texts (e.g., Wiki), we generate FAQ pairs from the formal and verbose rule and regulation documents, which is significant in real scenarios. To tackle this task, firstly, we carefully design a rules-based method to generate FAQ pairs based on structure information. Then we propose a pipeline framework for FAQ pair generation by deep learning. For experiments, we collect and annotate a Chinese FAQ pair generation dataset from documents of China Merchants Securities Co., Ltd. The results show that our method can generate proper FAQ pairs and achieve competitive performance in both automatic and human evaluation.

Keywords: Frequently asked question pair generation · Natural language processing · Deep learning

1 Introduction

With the development of deep learning and natural language processing, the progress of question-answer (QA) pair generation is notable. There are various research works about QA pair generation have been proposed. Among them, research on the frequently asked question (FAQ) pair generation task is one of the most appealing real-world application scenarios. In this work, we present a novel task to generate FAQ pairs from the rule and regulation documents. It will provide employers and customers with a convenient way to find the solution to their problems instead of reading plenty of documents. For a better illustration,

X. Pan et al. (Eds.): AIMS 2022, LNCS 13729, pp. 49–63, 2022.
https://doi.org/10.1007/978-3-031-23504-7_4

[Q]:信用账户可以资金调拨/归集吗？　(*Can funds be transferred/collected in a credit account?*)

[A]:不可以。信用账户只能关联一张银行卡，不存在多银行情况，因此无法操作资金调拨/资金归集。(*No. A credit account can only be associated with one bank card, and there is no multi-bank situation, so fund transfer/fund collection cannot be operated.*)

Fig. 1. Example FAQ pair from the corpus. Q and A refer to the question and the corresponding answer. Italic words in "()" are the English translation of the original Chinese texts on their left.

Fig. 1 shows one FAQ pair from our corpus as an example. The goal of our task is that given the well-written and detailed rule and regulation documents, the model can generate high-quality FAQ pairs from the document.

To date, previous works for QA pair generation focus on web texts, such as Wiki [4,10], online forums [5,15], etc. Moreover, they heavily rely on the existing machine reading comprehension dataset, such as SQuAD [8,14]. Even though great progress has been made in normal QA pair generation, the existing methods are therefore sub-optimal to handle FAQ pair generation for the rule and regulation document. The reason is three folds. First, the rule and regulation document is more formal than web texts and contains more terminology words. The gap in written style makes it hard to transfer previous methods to FAQ pair generation. Second, the structure of the document is well organized and can be used in FAQ generation. After we further analyze these kinds of documents, we find that 1) the document can be divided into proper passages using clue keywords, and 2) most of the sentences can be a pretty answer for the FAQ pair and can use to directly generate its corresponding questions. Last but not least, as shown in Fig. 1, the answer for the FAQ pair is long. In contrast, the answer for normal QA pair generation is short and covers few words. Furthermore, our work focus on FAQ pair generation about the rule and regulation documents from the finance and securities area, which is lack annotated corpus.

To tackle these challenges and make full use of the features of documents, we first annotate a Chinese dataset for FAQ pair generation on the rule and regulation document from China Merchants Securities Co., Ltd. Then, we mine the structure of these documents and design a series of rules for FAQ pair generation. Furthermore, to generate more natural and fluent FAQ pairs, a pipeline framework has been proposed, which is divided into two modules - Answer Extraction (AE) Model and Question Generation (QG) Model. The AE model is implemented as a combination model consisting of a sequence labeling model and a reading comprehension model, and we further tuned it for answers extraction of FAQ pairs. The QG model is designed based on the Chinese pre-trained model NEZHA [19] and UNILM [3] and can generate questions of FAQ pairs in various settings.

For a given document, we first split it into passages by the slide window method over the whole document. Each passage can contain multiple FAQ pairs. Then, we apply the AE model to the passage to extract the answer A. Afterward,

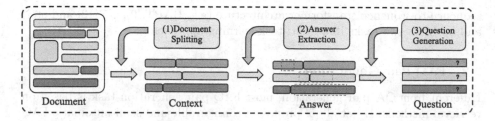

Fig. 2. Pipeline framework.

the answer A is concatenated with the passage and generates the question by the QG model. The architecture of our framework is illustrated in Fig. 2. Experiments show that our framework can achieve desirable performance compared to existing QA pair generation models. The human evaluation further demonstrates the capability of our framework to generate FAQ pairs from the rule and regulation document, fluent in language and diversity questions. We then do detailed ablation experiments to analyze the effectiveness of each component and the result prove that each part of our framework is important.

2 Related Work

2.1 QA Pair Generation

The generation of QA pairs is drawing growing attention in the NLP community. Most of the existing work focuses on generation QA pairs in a pipeline fashion. Du et al. [4] propose CorefNQG to solve QA pair generation problem. They first run the answer extraction module on the input text to obtain answers, and then run the question generation module to obtain the corresponding questions. Similarly, Willis et al. [20] generate Educational QA pair from the paragraph. Answer candidates (i.e. key phrases) from the paragraph context are first extracted, and then the questions are generated using the key phrases. Kumar et al. [8] use a three-stage system to generate QA pair. Except for the answer extraction module and question module, a question-answer module is introduced to validate the QA pairs. Shinoda et al. [14] present a variational QA pair generation model with explicit KL control to generate significantly diverse answers and questions. They assume that there are multiple latent QA pairs of a given paragraph and use a variational auto-encoder to control the diversifying of QA pairs. There are also studies focusing on generating QA pairs simultaneously. Tang et al. [17] combine the QA model and QG model to generate question and answer together. They explicitly leverage their probabilistic correlation as a regularization term to guide the training process of both models and achieve desirable performance. Cui et al. [2] point out that the pipeline method ignores the connection between question generation and answer extraction, which may lead to incompatible problems. Therefore, a model named OneStop is proposed to generate QA pairs in a one-stop approach. OneStop model uses canonical sequence-to-sequence transformer architecture (e.g. BART [9], T5 [13] and etc.) and optimize two tasks in a multi-task learning approach.

2.2   FAQ Pair Generation

Different from QA pair generation, most FAQ pair generation task is based on retrieval methods. Hu et al. [5] propose a configurable and semi-automatic FAQ finding process to construct the FAQ pairs in Open Source Project Forums. However, their method is not automatic and needs the forum managers to determine the final FAQ pairs. In [15], hierarchical agglomerative clustering is presented to get FAQ pairs from Student Question Answering Forums. They first exploit similarities between questions by using bag-of-words vectors and word embedding. Afterward, a hierarchical agglomerative clustering model is applied to cluster the questions into different groups and get the most frequently asked questions. This method only retrieves questions and focuses on specific areas in education. Bihani et al. [1] present a system to automatically generate education-specific FAQ pairs from Online Discussion Forums. The framework uses logistic regression and a random forest classifier to select past forums post for FAQ pairs and the experiments show that it can work well on multi-year forum datasets. The retrieval method has high requirements of data format and mostly tackles QA forums-type data. The generative method has been proposed in recent years for FAQ pairs generation. Raazaghi et al. [12] extend question-answering systems into the Auto-FAQGen-system to generate FAQ. This framework combines question extraction and question generation and can accept, extract, or generate user questions in order to create, maintain, and improve the quality of FAQ pairs. An architecture that performs end-to-end processing of the input text and displays QA pairs with the help of an automated QA generation pipeline is mentioned in [18]. The architecture consists of T5 for span extraction subsequent and question-answer generation, and a fine-tuned SpanBERT [7] for answer generation and ranking of the QA pairs. Furthermore, a knowledge graph is incorporated to gain additional domain knowledge. Jeyaraj et al. [6] proposes a novel F-Gen framework, which is an expert system that can generate potential FAQs from emails. The system is constituted of three subsystems: 1) query classifier subsystem for classific email texts; 2) FAQ group generator subsystem for generating FAQ pairs, and 3) FAQ generator subsystem for transforming email queries into FAQ pairs by clustering. Different from them, our work focuses on generating FAQ pairs from the rule and regulation documents and present a new framework that can generate FAQ pairs by the rule-based and generative-model-based method.

3   Data Collection and Analysis

3.1   Data Collection

Since there is no previous data for FAQ pair generation, we annotate a new dataset for this task. The raw rule and regulation documents come from China Merchants

Table 1. Statistics of our data.

	FAQ pairs num	Avg.question len	Avg.answer len	Avg.context len
Train	1073	20.47	71.28	499.89
Dev	135	21.79	90.52	564.53
Test	135	21.65	97.93	552.71

Securities Co., Ltd (i.e. CMS) and concentrate on the rules and regulations of stock trading. Here comes the step to annotating the data. First, we acquire 15 documents from CMS. Then, we assign one Chinese native speaker who is familiar with the finance area to tag the FAQ pairs following a series of rules. The annotation rules are 1) For sentences in the document with the potential to be an answer to FAQ pair, the annotator should use $< A_x >$ and $< /A_x >$ to tag it; 2) With the help of the tagged answer and context, the annotator should start with Q_y and write the frequently asked question corresponding to answer A_x; 3) The answer A_x can have multiple questions. Afterward, four partners check the quality of QA pairs and validate whether the QA pairs are FAQ pairs. QA pairs with poor quality and infrequency questions will be filtered out.

3.2 Data Analysis

After annotating and validating the data, we further analyze the data and show the details in Table 1. As seen, the length of answer is much longer than other QA pair generation tasks. This is caused by the properties of rule and regulation documents because this kind of document contains much more entities than simple documents, and this characteristic also makes our task more challenging.

[*Sentence*]:沪市开盘集合竞价时间为每个交易日的9:15至9:25。(*The opening call auction time of the Shanghai Stock Exchange is from 9:15 to 9:25 on each trading day.*)

[*Semantic Role Labeling*]:[$_{ARG0}$沪市开盘集合竞价时间] [$_{PRD}$为] [$_{ARG1}$每个交易日的9:15至9:25] ([$_{ARG0}$*The opening call auction time of the Shanghai Stock Exchange*] [$_{PRD}$*is*] [$_{ARG1}$*from 9:15 to 9:25 on each trading day*].)

[*Question*]:沪市开盘集合竞价时间为? (*When is the opening call auction time of the Shanghai Stock Exchange?*)

[*Answer*]:每个交易日的9:15至9:25 (*From 9:15 to 9:25 on each trading day*)

Fig. 3. Example from rule-based FAQ Pair generation. [$_{ARG0}$] and [$_{ARG1}$] mean causers and patient respectively. [$_{PRD}$] means the predicate. Italic words in "()" are the English translation of the original Chinese texts on their left.

4   Methodology

4.1   Rule-Based FAQ Pair Generation

Compared to web texts, the writing of rule and regulation documents is detailed, and the document structure is much more standardized. Moreover, these documents is focusing on stock trading which can help us to create meaningful FAQ pairs by simple rules.

FAQ Pair Generation Based-On Numerical Values. The rule and regulation documents exist a lot of sentences about numerical values, such as time, amount and number, etc. These expressions have a clear relation and we can use semantic role labeling to assign labels to words or phrases in a sentence that indicates their semantic role in the sentence.

Considering the example in Fig. 3, we first adopt the semantic role labeling to extract all semantic roles and their relation. Then we select the relation which contains both Causers or Experiencers $ARG0$ and Patient $ARG1$. At last, filtering the part of speech of word in $ARG1$ does not contain temporal nouns. Based on this, we can utilize the $ARG0$ and PRD to generate the question about the numerical answer by connecting them and adding question marks. For the integrity of question, the position of other roles in sentence locating between $ARG0$ and PRD will add to the final question. Inspired by the power of LTP tool[1], both the semantic role labeling and part of speech methods all use LTP tool.

[*Segment*]:1.竞价时间:沪市开盘集合竞价时间为每个交易日的9:15至9:25。(*The opening call auction time:The opening call auction time of the Shanghai Stock Exchange is from 9:15 to 9:25 on each trading day.*)

[*Keywords*]:沪市开盘，竞价时间 (*The opening call auction of the Shanghai Stock Exchange, The opening call auction time*)

[*Verb phrases*]:竞价(*The opening call auction of the Shanghai Stock Exchange*)
[*Noun phrases*]:竞价时间(*The opening call auction time*)

[*Question*]:沪市开盘业务的竞价时间具体是什么？(*When is the opening call auction time of the Shanghai Stock Exchange?*)
[*Answer*]:沪市开盘集合竞价时间为每个交易日的9:15至9:25。(*The opening call auction time of the Shanghai Stock Exchange is from 9:15 to 9:25 on each trading day.*)

Fig. 4. Verb and Noun phrases are extracted by POS tool of LTP from the last keyword of the sentence.

---

[1] https://github.com/HIT-SCIR/ltp.

[*prefix*]:什么是A，如何解释A，……(*What is A, How to explain A*)
[*suffix*]:A具体是什么，A定义是什么，……(*A 's concrete meaning, A 's definition*)

Fig. 5. Modifiers of Noun phrases.

[*prefix*]:如何操作A，如何进行A，……(*How to use A, How to do A*)
[*suffix*]:A具体的操作流程，A可以如何完成，……(*A 's procedure, How to finish A*)

Fig. 6. Modifiers of Verb phrases.

FAQ Pair Generation Based-On Keywords. Since documents are organized in clear structure by titles and sub-titles, we could extract the keywords of the article and split them into multiple segments, as shown in Fig. 4. The keywords represent the general meaning of those segments. We build FAQ pairs based on the keywords and the segments.

Because the last keyword is usually the nearest title of the part and the most specific summarization, we construct the question based on the POS information of the last keyword of one part. We prepared two kinds of modifiers for Noun and Verb phrases respectively, as shown in Fig. 5 and Fig. 6. Then we concatenate the modifiers and the keywords to obtain the questions.

4.2 Pipeline Framework

In this section, we first make an overall description of our pipeline framework. Then to better understand the core component of our framework, we also make a detailed illustration of the Answer Extraction Modular and the Question Generation Modular.

Overall Framework. As illustrated in Fig. 2, our pipeline framework mainly consists of three stages. Firstly, given the document D, we split it to get various contexts $\{C_1, C_2, ..., C_n\}$ by the simple slide windows method over the whole document. Secondly, for each context, we use an answer extraction modular to extract fine-grained answers $\{a_1, a_2, ..., a_m\}$ from corresponding context. Then in the last stage, we use the combined information of extracted answers and the corresponding context to generate question $\{q_1, q_2, ..., q_m\}$ by a question generation modular. Through this pipeline, the QA pair $\{(q_1, a_1), (q_2, a_2), ..., (q_m, a_m)\}$ can be generated from document.

Answer Extraction Modular. Given the context split from document, the Answer Extraction modular extracts fine-grained answers from it. As shown in Fig. 7, the answer extraction modular's backbone is a sequence labeling model for answer tagging. Though the simple sequence labeling method faces two main problems in our task: (1) The paragraph in rule and regulation document is more

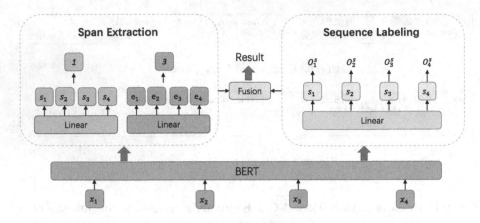

Fig. 7. Answer extraction.

formal and is full of entities, which means there is not only an answer worthy of being extracted. Nevertheless, the extraction result will be relatively single for a single sequence labeling model; (2) The answer in our task is longer than other tasks and the special written style of rule and regulation document is more difficult to understand, which makes the sequence labeling task more challenging, however, the amount of our collect dataset is limited, which is difficult to do full training. We use two approaches to improve these two problems relatively. Firstly, we combine the sequence labeling results with another machine reading comprehension model's result inspired by [16]. And we set these two models using a pre-trained language model as sharing encoder and learning in a multi-task way, which can be formulated as:

$$L = L_{NER} + L_{Span} \tag{1}$$

where L_{NER} is the sequence labeling model's loss and L_{Span} is the machine reading comprehension model's loss. Compared with the single sequence labeling model's result, the fused result from two kinds of models will be much more sufficient. Secondly, we make a pre-training step on other Chinese QA datasets (e.g. SogouQA) before the finetune stage, because the parametric knowledge obtained from pretraining could be beneficial to the downstream answer extraction task.

Question Generation Modular. The Question Generation modular aims to generate the corresponding question for a given answer and context. As shown in Fig. 8, the question generation modular applies UNILM model and adopts NEZHA pre-trained model to initialize the parameter of UNILM. Two reasons make these chosen: (1) the question generation task generally adopts the Seq-to-Seq model, including generative models such as T5, BART, and the unified language model UNILM. However, the current generative models commonly use the English or multilingual corpus to train the language model, which does not

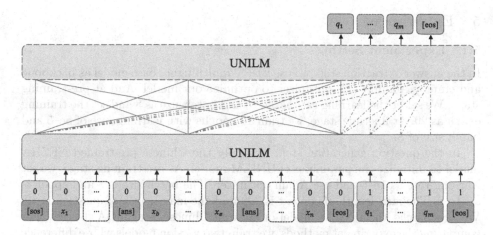

Fig. 8. Question geneartion.

match our Chinese task. To fill this gap, we attention that the UNILM model can use the parameter of BERT and there are many BERT models, which apply Chinese corpus to pretrain, including Chinese-BERT-wwm, ERNIE-baidu, NEZHA, etc. (2) due to the experiments from NEZHA paper, the NEZHA model is better than Chinese-BERT-wwm and ERNIE-baidu models.

However, the simple UNILM model exists two problems in our task: (1) due to the limitation of dataset size, there are only 1343 pieces of data. The model has a slow convergence speed and weak generalization ability. (2) the input data context is gained by slide windows. This method will make the context obtaining some redundant information. We apply two approaches to improve these two problems respectively. Firstly, we make a pre-training step on another Chinese QA dataset (SogouQA) before the finetune stage. Secondly, we add special tokens both before and after of answer. This method not only labels the position of answer, but contains the information of context.

As shown in Fig. 8, the input of model is the concatenation of context c with the special token labeling, and the output is to generate the question q. The cross-entropy loss for question generation is:

$$L_{qg} = -\sum_{t=1}^{m} \log P\left(q_t \mid q_{<m}, c; \theta\right) \tag{2}$$

where m is the length of question and $P\left(q_t \mid q_{<m}, c; \theta\right)$ is the predicted probability of q_t. c is denoted as: $c = \{[sos]C_1, C_2, ..., C_b, [special\ token], C_b + 1, C_b + 2, ..., C_e, [special\ token], C_e + 1, C_e + 2, ..., C_n[eos]\}$.

5 Experiment

5.1 Experiment Setting

In the answer extraction step, we use BERT multilingual base model as backbone and employ AdamW [11] optimizer to optimize our model. And at pre-training stage, We select the learning rate as 5e—5 and batch size as 8 and set the training epoch as 20. At finetune stage, we train 10 epochs with learning rate of 5e–5 and batch size of 8.

In the question generation step, we apply the Chinese pre-trained NEZHA model to initialize the parameter of UNILM model. At pre-training stage, we set learning rate as 1e–5 and use Adam optimizer. The batch size is 8 and epoch is set to 8. The max length of context is 300 and the max length of question is 80. We pre-trained the UNILM model on a large Chinese SougouQA dataset. For comparing the experiment methods, we train two version models whose difference is that the input sentence with the special token or not. At finetune stage, we use the same learning rate, Adam optimizer, batch size, the max length of context, and question, but the epoch is set to 20.

The total experiment is run with Tesla V100 GPUs and in all of our experiments, we save the model making best performance on validation dataset then test it on the test dataset.

5.2 Evaluation Metrics

In this section, we make a detailed description of the evaluation metrics of our experiment.

Answer Extraction Evaluation. We chose $Precision$, $Recall$, and $F1-score$ as the evaluation metrics to evaluate the result of answer extraction modular and the ground-truth answers.

Question Generation Evaluation. The question generation modular adopts $Rouge-1$, $Rouge-2$, $Rouge-l$, $BLEU$, $BLEU-1$ and $BLEU-2$ as the evaluation metrics to evaluate between the generated questions and the ground-truth questions.

Question-Answer Pairs Evaluation. To our knowledge, there is no standard metric to evaluate the score of QA Pairs. We apply the method of human annotation to gain the score for every QA Pair. Concretely, we evaluate the quality of the QA pair on three conventional criteria: Relevance, Fluency and Integrity in perspective of QA pair, question and answer, respectively. And these are rated on a three-scale as follows:

- Score 0: indicates the generation quality is unacceptable.
- Score 1: expresses the generation quality is moderate or unsure to decide.
- Score 2: represents the generation quality is excellent performance.

Table 2. The ablation result of answer extraction. BERT+NER stands for the base sequence labeling model. +Span means the combination with machine reading comprehension model. +Pretrained representatives performing pre-train before finetuning.

	Precision	Recall	F1-score
BERT+NER	42.42	22.43	22.50
+Span	57.39	43.19	42.70
+Pretrained	59.23	45.07	44.85
+Span+Pretrained	**60.78**	**47.43**	**47.70**

Table 3. The ablation result of question generation. NEZHA+UNILM stands for sequence to sequence model. +Pretrained means performing pre-trained before finetuning. +[special token] representatives the special token is added both before and after of answer. +Pretrained+[special token] combines the above two improvements.

	Rouge-1	Rouge-2	Rouge-L	BLEU	BLEU-1	BLEU-2
NEZHA+UNILM	49.03	32.36	45.95	22.95	39.04	27.30
+Pretrained	50.48	33.80	47.12	24.32	40.49	28.69
+[special token]	60.63	44.93	57.00	34.24	50.45	39.04
+Pretrained+[special token]	**64.46**	**49.51**	**61.63**	**39.55**	**55.32**	**44.06**

5.3 Analysis Experiment

Answer Extraction. To verify the effectiveness of our Answer Extraction Modular, we remove the two improvements to observe their effectiveness. From the results shown in Table 2, We have the following observations: (1) The simple sequence labeling method's performance is not satisfactory. This indicated that our task is more challenging than the existing QA pair generation task. (2) With the combination of another machine reading comprehension model's result, the answer extraction result is obviously improved by making a large margin of 20.20%, 14.97% and 20.76% improvement at F1-score, precision and recall, respectively. We attribute it to the fact that the combination approach can extract various of answer than the single model and the diversity of answers is important for our proposed task. (3) It is apparent that after doing pre-training based on the sequence labeling model, all the metrics will be pushed to better performance. Concretely, 22.35%, 16.81% and 22.64% improvements are made at F1-score, precision and recall respectively compared with the backbone model. This represents that pre-trained approach successfully gives the model more knowledge in answer extraction task. (4) Based on the combination model, the pretrained method can also bring further improvement to answer extraction, which beats the combination model by 5.00% at F1-score, 3.39% at precision and 4.24% recall. This suggests that pre-trained approach can also contribute to the combination model and further verified its effectiveness.

Table 4. Result of human evaluation from four methods. Numerical Values-Based and Keywords Based are two rule-based methods to generate FAQ pairs. Based Pipeline means the composition of the answer extraction modular using BERT+NER method and the question generation modular adopting NEZHA+UNILM approach. Similarly, Improved Pipeline represents the composition of +Span+Pretrained and +Pretrained+[special token] methods.

Method	Answer quality	Question quality	QA quality
Rule-based method			
Numerical Values Based	1.71	1.43	1.40
Keywords Based	1.89	1.76	1.58
Pipeline Framework			
Based Pipeline	1.47	1.75	0.86
Improved Pipeline	1.70	1.82	1.48

Question Generation. We make ablation experiments to explore the effectiveness of the two improvements to prove the performance of our Question Generation Modular. The result is displayed in Table 3. The experimental result is that if the NEZHA+UNILM model is directly used, the Rouge-L and BLEU are only 45.95 and 22.95 respectively. As we can see from the table, both two improvements are effective, especially adding special tokens. It significantly outperforms the NEZHA+UNILM model with 11.05 and 11.29 absolute points with respect to Rouge-L and BLEU metrics respectively. The reason is that the special token method can contain the context information while labeling the position of the answer. Compared with adding special token method, the combination of pre-trained and adding special token methods can gain further improvement. This show that using the relevant large dataset makes pre-trained is contributed to the question generation task during the dataset of task is limited.

5.4   Human Evaluation

We further analyze the QA pair's quality generated by our overall pipeline framework. Specifically, we hair three experts who were trained in advance to annotate our QA pair generation results. Then we average their scoring results in our three-scale way as the final score of human evaluation. Results are shown in Table 4, it is easy to observe that the two rule-based methods proposed by us are fairly efficient and reach high performance in our three-scale scoring way. We can also observe that our based pipeline method's performance is unsatisfactory. We attribute it to the reason that our task is more difficult than other QA pair generation tasks, therefore, although the based pipeline method already makes promising results in the common QA pair generation task, direct use of it will not achieve good results in our tasks. Another interesting observation is that our improved pipeline method makes much better performance compared with the based pipeline method. This suggests that our proposed improvements effectively tackle the challenges of our FAQ pair generation task for the rule and regulation document.

5.5 Case Study

To further explain why our proposed method works, we provide a case study made on our improved pipeline framework and two rule-based methods. To better show why our framework is effective, we also provide a QA pair generated by the base pipeline framework. As shown in Table 5, the result of the two rule-based methods' generation is excellent and these two approaches are generated from different perspectives, which makes our results full of variety. We can also observe that compared with the base pipeline framework generating incomplete and irrelevant answers, our best pipeline framework could do well on our task by a satisfactory generation. This further verifies the improvement is suitable for our proposed task. Another interesting observation is that our two rule-based methods and pipeline framework can generate various QA pairs from different viewpoints, making the generation result more diverse and sufficient.

Table 5. Question-Answer Pairs Cases. The four lines examples namely 1,2,3 and 4 are generated by Numerical Values-Based, Keywords Based, Based Pipeline, and Improved Pipeline methods, respectively.

1	[Q]:单笔买卖申报最大数量不得超过? (*Exceeded the maximum number of single-buy submissions?*) [A]:30万股 (*300,000 shares*)
2	[Q]:北交所新股网上发行规则中网上申购费用一般是多少? (*What is the general online subscription fee in the rules for online issuance of new shares of the Beijing Stock Exchange?*) [A]:11、网上申购费用; 北交所新股网上申购无费用 (*11. Online subscription fee; There is no fee for online subscription of new shares on the Beijing Stock Exchange.*)
3	[Q]:网上申购新股是? (*What is the online subscription of new shares?*) [A]: (1) 我司渠道 (*(1)The channel of our Company*)
4	[Q]:创业板交易的新规规定退市整理期是? (*What is the delisting adjustment period stipulated by the new regulations for GEM trading?*) [A]:退市整理期的交易期限为十五个交易日。 (*The trading period of the delisting arrangement period is fifteen trading days.*)

6 Conclusion

In this paper, we propose a novel and challenging task to generate frequently asked question (FAQ) pairs for the rule and regulation document and contribute a Chinese annotated dataset. Due to the character of our collected data, we design two rule-based methods and a pipeline framework. Experimental results on our dataset show that both the rule-based method and the pipeline framework can generate high-quality QA pairs from the document. We hope our task can facilitate future research in the question-answering field.

Acknowledgments. This work was partially supported by the National Natural Science Foundation of China (62006062, 62176076), Shenzhen Foundational Research Funding JCYJ20200109113441941, Shenzhen Key Technology Project JSGG20210802154400001 and Joint Lab of HITSZ and China Merchants Securities.

References

1. Bihani, A., Ullman, J.D., Paepcke, A.: FAQtor?: automatic FAQ generation using online forums. Tech. rep, Stanford InfoLab (2018)
2. Cui, S., et al.: Onestop qamaker: extract question-answer pairs from text in a one-stop approach. CoRR abs/2102.12128 (2021)
3. Dong, L., et al.: Unified language model pre-training for natural language understanding and generation. In: Wallach, H.M., Larochelle, H., Beygelzimer, A., d'Alché-Buc, F., Fox, E.B., Garnett, R. (eds.) Advances in Neural Information Processing Systems 32: Annual Conference on Neural Information Processing Systems 2019, NeurIPS 2019, 8–14 December 2019, Vancouver, BC, Canada, pp. 13042–13054 (2019)
4. Du, X., Cardie, C.: Harvesting paragraph-level question-answer pairs from wikipedia. In: Gurevych, I., Miyao, Y. (eds.) Proceedings of the 56th Annual Meeting of the Association for Computational Linguistics, ACL 2018, Melbourne, Australia, 15–20 July 2018, Vol. 1: Long Paper, pp. 1907–1917. Association for Computational Linguistics (2018)
5. Hu, W., Yu, D., Jiau, H.C.: A FAQ finding process in open source project forums. In: Hall, J.G., Kaindl, H., Lavazza, L., Buchgeher, G., Takaki, O. (eds.) The Fifth International Conference on Software Engineering Advances, ICSEA 2010, 22–27 August 2010, Nice, France, pp. 259–264. IEEE Computer Society (2010)
6. Jeyaraj, S.T.R.: A deep learning based end-to-end system (F-GEN) for automated email FAQ generation. Expert Syst. Appl. **187**, 115896 (2022)
7. Joshi, M., Chen, D., Liu, Y., Weld, D.S., Zettlemoyer, L., Levy, O.: Spanbert: improving pre-training by representing and predicting spans. Trans. Assoc. Comput. Linguistics **8**, 64–77 (2020)
8. Kumar, A., Kharadi, A., Singh, D., Kumari, M.: Automatic question-answer pair generation using deep learning. In: 2021 Third International Conference on Inventive Research in Computing Applications (ICIRCA) (2021)
9. Lewis, M., et al.: BART: denoising sequence-to-sequence pre-training for natural language generation, translation, and comprehension. In: Jurafsky, D., Chai, J., Schluter, N., Tetreault, J.R. (eds.) Proceedings of the 58th Annual Meeting of the Association for Computational Linguistics, ACL 2020, Online, 5–10 July 2020, pp. 7871–7880. Association for Computational Linguistics (2020)
10. Li, Z., Wang, W., Dong, L., Wei, F., Xu, K.: Harvesting and refining question-answer pairs for unsupervised QA. In: Jurafsky, D., Chai, J., Schluter, N., Tetreault, J.R. (eds.) Proceedings of the 58th Annual Meeting of the Association for Computational Linguistics, ACL 2020, Online, 5–10 July 2020, pp. 6719–6728. Association for Computational Linguistics (2020)

11. Loshchilov, I., Hutter, F.: Decoupled weight decay regularization. In: International Conference on Learning Representations (2019)
12. Raazaghi, F.: Auto-FAQ-Gen: automatic frequently asked questions generation. In: Barbosa, D., Milios, E. (eds.) CANADIAN AI 2015. LNCS (LNAI), vol. 9091, pp. 334–337. Springer, Cham (2015). https://doi.org/10.1007/978-3-319-18356-5_30
13. Raffel, C., et al.: Exploring the limits of transfer learning with a unified text-to-text transformer. J. Mach. Learn. Res. **21**, 140:1–140:67 (2020)
14. Shinoda, K., Sugawara, S., Aizawa, A.: Improving the robustness of QA models to challenge sets with variational question-answer pair generation. In: Kabbara, J., Lin, H., Paullada, A., Vamvas, J. (eds.) Proceedings of the ACL-IJCNLP 2021 Student Research Workshop, ACL 2021, Online, 5–10 July 2021, pp. 197–214. Association for Computational Linguistics (2021)
15. Sindhgatta, R., Marvaniya, S., Dhamecha, T.I., Sengupta, B.: Inferring frequently asked questions from student question answering forums. In: Hu, X., Barnes, T., Hershkovitz, A., Paquette, L. (eds.) Proceedings of the 10th International Conference on Educational Data Mining, EDM 2017, Wuhan, Hubei, China, 25–28 June 2017. International Educational Data Mining Society (IEDMS) (2017)
16. Son, N.H., Vu, H.M., Nguyen, T.A.D., Nguyen, M.L.: Jointly learning span extraction and sequence labeling for information extraction from business documents. ArXiv abs/2205.13434 (2022)
17. Tang, D., Duan, N., Qin, T., Zhou, M.: Question answering and question generation as dual tasks. CoRR abs/1706.02027 (2017)
18. Vasisht, S., Tirthani, V., Eppa, A., Koujalgi, P., Srinath, R.: Automatic FAQ generation using text-to-text transformer model. In: 2022 3rd International Conference for Emerging Technology (INCET) (2022)
19. Wei, J., et al.: NEZHA: neural contextualized representation for Chinese language understanding. CoRR abs/1909.00204 (2019)
20. Willis, A., Davis, G.M., Ruan, S., Manoharan, L., Landay, J.A., Brunskill, E.: Key phrase extraction for generating educational question-answer pairs. In: Proceedings of the Sixth ACM Conference on Learning @ Scale, L@S 2019, Chicago, IL, USA, 24–25 June 2019, pp. 20:1–20:10. ACM (2019)

Chinese Text Classification Using BERT and Flat-Lattice Transformer

Haifeng Lv[1,3], Yishuang Ning[2(✉)], Ke Ning[2], Xiaoyu Ji[1,3], and Sheng He[2]

[1] Guangxi Key Laboratory of Machine Vision and Intelligent Control, WuZhou University, Wuzhou, China
[2] Kingdee Research, Kingdee International Software Group Company Limited, Shenzhen, China
ningyishuang@126.com
[3] Guangxi Colleges and Universities Key Laboratory of Industry Software Technology, Wuzhou University, Wuzhou 543002, China

Abstract. Recently, large scale pre-trained language models such as BERT and models with lattice structure that consisting of character-level and word-level information have achieved state-of-the-art performance in most downstream natural language processing (NLP) tasks, including named entity recognition (NER), English text classification and sentiment analysis. For Chinese text classification, the existing methods have also tried such kinds of models. However, they cannot obtain the desired results since these pre-trained models are based on characters, which cannot be applied for Chinese language that is based on words. To address this problem, in this paper, we propose BFLAT which a simple but efficient model for Chinese text classification. Specifically, BFLAT utilizes BERT and word2vec to learn character-level and word-level vector representations, and then adopts the flat-lattice transformer to integrate both of the two-level vector representations. Experimental results on two datasets demonstrate that our proposed method outperforms the baseline methods over 1.38–21.82% and 3.42–20.7% in terms of relative F1-measure on two Chinese text classification benchmarks, respectively.

Keywords: Chinese text classification · BERT · Flat-lattice transformer · Embedding representation

1 Introduction

Text classification plays an import role in most downstream natural language processing (NLP) [1, 2] tasks. It is defined to tag the given text with a predefined set of labels. The recent popularity of neural networks has sparked interest in neural text classification models [3–5].

For Chinese language without natural separators, approaches based on English language could not be utilized directly. Most existing methods for Chinese text classification are based on word-level [6–8], which firstly requires to adopt NLP tools for word segmentation. However, the mistakes caused by these segmentation tools may influence the effectiveness of the Chinese text classification task.

Recently, lattice structure has shown great potential for exploiting word information and avoiding word segmentation error propagation [9, 10]. By matching a sentence with a lexicon, the lattice can be obtained. As shown in Fig. 1(a), the lattice is a directed acyclic graph (DAG) consisting of multiple nodes, where each node is a latent word or a character in the sentence. They are not in order, the first and last characters of the word determine their positions. Besides, some words in the lattice may be important for text classification. For example, in Fig. 1(a), "人和医院(Renhe Hospital)" can be utilized to make a distinction between the city "北京(Beijing)" and the people "北京人(Beijing People)".

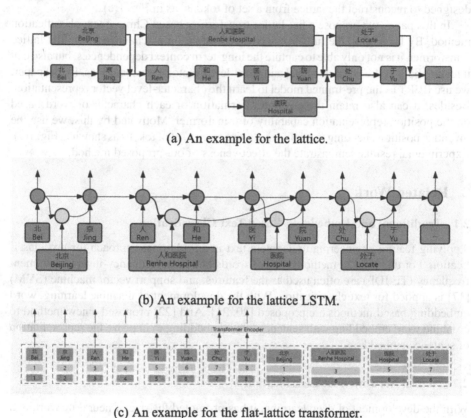

(a) An example for the lattice.

(b) An example for the lattice LSTM.

(c) An example for the flat-lattice transformer.

Fig. 1. Examples for the lattice, the lattice LSTM and the flat-lattice transformer. In 1(c) ▓, ▓, ▓, indicates tokens, heads and tails, respectively. (Color figure online)

There are three ways to adopt the lattice. The first way is to construct a model which is compatible with lattice input, such as lattice LSTM [9] and LR-CNN [11]. In the lattice LSTM, an extra word cell is applied to encode the latent words, and attention mechanism is used to integrate variable-number nodes at each position, as in Fig. 1(b). LR-CNN adopts convolutional neural network (CNN) to encode latent words in different window sizes. However, CNN and RNN are difficult to capture long-term dependencies, which are useful for text classification. Besides, the dynamic lattice structure used in these methods cannot fully leverage the parallel computing capability of the Graphic Processing Unit (GPU). The second way is to transform lattice into graph and use the graph neural network (GNN) to encode it, such as lexicon-based graph network (LGN) [12] and collaborative graph network (CGN) [13]. While sequential structure is still important for text classification and graph is general counterpart, their gap is not negligible. These models require to use LSTM as the bottom encoder to carry the sequential inductive bias, which makes the model complex. The third way is to convert the lattice structure into a flat structure consisting of spans, such as flat lattice transformer proposed by [14], in which the ingenious position encoding for the lattice structure is designed to reconstruct the lattice from a set of tokens, as in Fig. 1(c).

In this paper, we propose a flat-lattice transformer based Chinese text classification method. By leveraging the fully-connected self-attention mechanism of the flat-lattice transformer, it is not only able to capture the long-term context dependencies, but also can integrate both of the character-level and word-level vector representations. In this paper, we use BERT as the pre-trained model to learn the character-level vector representation. Besides, it can also retain the position information of each character or word based on the position representation capability of transformer. Motivated by this, we use the inventive position encoding to rebuild the lattice from a set of tokens as shown in Fig. 1(c). Experimental results demonstrate the effectiveness of our proposed method.

2   Related Work

2.1   Traditional and Embedding-Based Text Classification

Applying feature engineering to denote a text is a traditional approach for text classification. For this kind of methods, bag of words and term frequency-inverse document frequency (TF-IDF) are often used as the features, and support vector machine (SVM) [17] is applied for text classification. With the development of machine learning, word embedding based methods are proposed [20, 21]. And [22] proposed a new method to combine word embedding with sentence label embedding to improve the representation of sentence embedding.

2.2   Neural Network Text Classification

With the development of deep learning, it has promoted the rise of neural network text classification where CNN and RNN based models are often utilized. For instance, [23] proposed a CNN-based sentence classification model. [24] and [25] proposed a deep pyramid word-level CNN and character-level CNN to excavate different level information in the sentence, respectively. [26, 27] used LSTM which is an extended form of RNN to learn contextual representation. To integrate extra information in the sentence, attention mechanism [28] is designed to produce text representations via a more flexible way. Other studies used novel neural networks like GCN [29] and CapsuleNet [30] to encode sequences for classification. Besides, there were also some researchers that used the pre-trained language models such as ALBERT and XLNet for text classification. Although these methods can achieve good results in the English language, they cannot be applied to the Chinese language directly due to the inherent differences with English.

2.3 Chinese Text Classification

Most current Chinese text classification approaches were nearly character-based or word-based. To integrate both of the character-level and word-level information, [8] utilized two detached bidirectional LSTM (BLSTM) models to obtain the character-level and word-level features, respectively, and then combined them for Chinese text classification. To reduce the segmentation error, [9] proposed a lattice LSTM for Chinese named entity recognition. Lattice LSTM clearly used character and word information via several gates, which control to choose most related characters and words from one sentence. This sequence labeling method was also applied to the task of Chinese word segmentation [33], which achieved superior results on several benchmarks.

2.4 Transformer Related Theory

In this section, we simply present the transformer architecture. Focusing on the Chinese text classification task, we just took over the transformer encoder. The transformer encoder consists of a self-attention layer and a feed forward network (FFN) layer. Each sub-layer is followed by residual connection and layer normalization. FFN is a position-wise multi-layer Perceptron with nonlinear transformation. Transformer performs self-attention over the sequence by H heads of attention individually and then concatenates the result of H heads. For simplicity, we omitted the head index in the formula below. The result of each head is computed as:

$$\mathrm{Att}(\mathbf{A},\mathbf{V}) = \mathrm{softmax}(\mathbf{A})\mathbf{V} \tag{1}$$

$$\mathbf{A}_{\mathrm{ij}} = \left(\frac{Q_i K_j^{\mathsf{T}}}{\sqrt{d_{head}}}\right) \tag{2}$$

$$[\mathrm{Q,K,V}] = E_x[\mathbf{W}_q, \mathbf{W}_k, \mathbf{W}_v] \tag{3}$$

where E is the token embedding lookup table or the output of final Transformer layer. $\mathbf{W}_q, \mathbf{W}_k, \mathbf{W}_v \in \mathbb{R}^{d_{\mathrm{mod}\,el} \times d_{head}}$ are learnable parameters, and $d_{\mathrm{mod}\,el} = H \times d_{head}$, d_{head} is the dimension of each head. The vanilla transformer also utilized absolute position encoding to catch the sequential information. Inspired by the model proposed by [34], we consider the commutativity of the vector inner dot would lead to the loss of directionality in self-attention. Therefore, the relative position of our adopted lattice is also important for Chinese text classification.

3 Approaches

Figure 2 depicts the overall architecture of the proposed flat-lattice transformer based Chinese text classification approach. The architecture is composed of four layers: the input layer, the embedding layer, the encoder layer and the output layer. Firstly, in the input layer, the input sentence is processed to obtain its character sequence, lexicon sequence and their respective start position and end position. Secondly, in the embedding layer, for the character sequence, we use large-scale pre-trained language models (e.g. BERT, ALBERT, RoBERTa and ERNIE) to generate its character-level vector representation (We use BERT in this paper); For the lexicon sequence, we use word2vec to acquire the word-level vector representation. Then, both of the character-level and word-level vector representations are represented as a lattice in Fig. 1(c) which is sent to the transformer model with relative position encoding to obtain the sentence-level feature vector of the input sentence in the encoder layer. Finally, the sentence-level feature vector is sent to the output layer to get the classification category with the Softmax function.

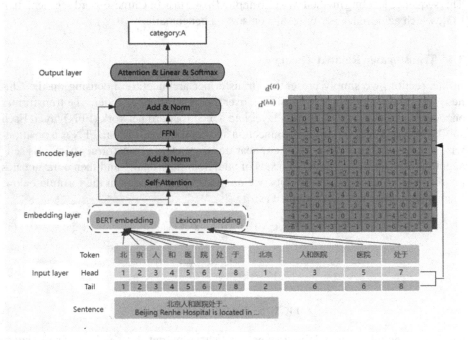

Fig. 2. The overall architecture of BFLAT.

3.1 Converting Lattice into Flat Structure

We flatten the lattice after obtaining a lattice from the character-level and word-level vector representations. The flat lattice can be regarded as a set of spans, where each span corresponds to a token, a head and a tail, as in Fig. 1(c), designed by [14]. The token is a character or a word. The head and tail represent the position index of the token's first and last characters in the input sentence, respectively. For the character, its head and tail are the same. There is a simple algorithm to reinstate the flat-lattice into its original structure. We first take the token which has the same head and tail to create a character sequence. Then we use other tokens (words) with their heads and tails to build skip-paths. Since our transformation is recoverable, we suppose the flat-lattice can keep the original structure of lattice.

3.2 Relative Position Encoding of Spans

The flat-lattice structure is composed of spans with different sizes. To encode the inter-actions among spans, we adopt the relative position encoding of spans [14]. Specifically, for two spans x_i and x_j in a lattice, there are three kinds of relationships which are decided by their heads and tails between them: intersection, inclusion and separation. Instead of directly encoding these relationships, we use a dense vector to build their relations which are computed by continuous transformation of the head and tail information. Therefore, we consider that it cannot only denote the relation between two tokens, but also show more detailed information such as the distance between a character and a word. Let $head[i]$ and $tail[i]$ denote the head and tail position of span x_i, respectively. We utilize two kinds of relative distances to denote the relation between x_i and x_j. They can be computed as:

$$d_{ij}^{(hh)} = head[i] - head[j] \tag{4}$$

$$d_{ij}^{(tt)} = tail[i] - tail[j] \tag{5}$$

where $d_{ij}^{(hh)}$ represents the distance between the head of x_i and x_j, and $d_{ij}^{(tt)}$ is the distance between the tail of x_i and x_j. A simple non-linear transformation of the two distances is viewed as the final relative position encoding of spans:

$$R_{ij} = \text{ReLU}(W_r(\text{p}_{d_{ij}^{(hh)}} \oplus \text{p}_{d_{ij}^{(tt)}})) \tag{6}$$

where W_r is a learnable parameter, $\oplus$ represents the concatenation operator, and p_d is calculated as in [16],

$$\text{p}_d^{(2\kappa)} = \sin\left(d/10000^{2\kappa/d \bmod el}\right) \tag{7}$$

$$\text{p}_d^{(2\kappa+1)} = \cos\left(d/10000^{2\kappa/d \bmod el}\right) \tag{8}$$

where d is $d_{ij}^{(hh)}$ and $d_{ij}^{(tt)}$, respectively, and κ denotes the index of dimension of position encoding. Then we utilize a variant self-attention [35] to exploit the relative span position encoding as follows:

$$\begin{aligned} \mathbf{A}_{i,j}^* = & W_q^T E_{x_i}^T E_{x_j} W_{k,E} + W_q^T E_{x_i}^T R_{ij} W_{k,R} \\ & + \mathbf{u}^T E_{x_j} W_{k,E} + \mathbf{v}^T R_{ij} W_{k,R} \end{aligned} \tag{9}$$

where $W_q, W_{\kappa,R}, W_{\kappa,E} \in \mathbb{R}^{d \bmod el \times d_{head}}$ and u,v $\in \mathbb{R}^{d_{head}}$ are learnable parameters. Then we exchange A with A* in Eq. (1). The following calculation is consistent with the original Transformer.

3.3 Classifier and Optimization

After obtaining the sequence of hidden vectors by the flat-lattice transformer encoder, we put it into a character-level attention module to generate the sentence-level feature vectors represented as $g \in \mathbb{R}^{d_h}$, where d_h is the dimension of hidden vectors. The last representation g is the weighted sum of the hidden vector sequence:

$$g = \sum_{i=1}^{m} u_i \cdot \mathbf{h}_i, \tag{10}$$

$$u_i = \frac{\mathbf{v}' \mathbf{h}_i}{\sum_{k=1}^{m} \mathbf{v}' \mathbf{h}_k}, \tag{11}$$

where $\mathbf{v} \in \mathbb{R}^{d_h}$ is a trainable parameter. We choose this form of attention because it can achieve better performance among several alternatives.

Then g is fed into a fully-connected layer to calculate the confidence score of each category:

$$\mathbf{o} = \mathbf{w}_o g + \mathbf{b}_o, \tag{12}$$

where $\mathbf{w}_o \in \mathbb{R}^{K \times d_h}$ is a learnable weighted matrix, $\mathbf{b}_o \in \mathbb{R}^K$ is a bias term, and K denotes the number of text categories. The probability of text s belongs to category y is calculated as:

$$p(y|s) = \frac{\exp(o_y)}{\sum_{i=1}^{K} \exp(o_i)}, \tag{13}$$

And the cross-entropy loss is selected as our objective function. Given the training data set $T = \{(s^i, y^i)\}$, the loss is calculated as:

$$J(\Theta) = - \sum_{i=1}^{|T|} \log p(y^i|s^i; \Theta) \tag{14}$$

where Θ represents all parameters utilized in the proposed model. During the implementation, we utilize stochastic gradient descent (SGD) to minimize the loss function iteratively until convergence.

4 Experiments

4.1 Experimental Setup

Datasets. In order to evaluate the effectiveness of our proposed method, we use two Chinese datasets which can be seen in Table 1. The first dataset[1] is collected from Chinese news titles with 32 categories, where 47, 952 titles are viewed as training set, and 15, 986 for testing [8] (i.e., # Dataset 1). The second dataset is a benchmark on Chinese CLUE[2] (i.e., # Dataset 2), which includes 53, 360 sentences for training, 10,000 sentences for validation, and 10, 000 sentences for testing.

Table 1. Two Chinese datasets details.

Dataset	Training	Validation	Testing
Dataset 1	47,952	–	15,986
Dataset 2	53,360	10,000	10,000

Evaluation Metrics. In the experiment, we utilize accuracy (ACC), macro-precision (P), macro-recall (R) and macro-F1-score to evaluate the performance of Chinese text classification. **Hyper-parameters optimization of the BFLAT model**. We set the hyper-parameters of the proposed model to obtain the best results. Table 2 lists the hyper-parameters obtained from the development experiment of Dataset 1 and Dataset 2. In particular, we adopt the one-layer Transformer encoder for proposed model. For word-based competitors in our experiments, we use jieba[3] segmentation tool to cut Chinese texts into word sequences.

Table 2. Hyper-parameters for BFLAT model.

Name	Value
lr	1e−3
decay	0.05
optimizer	SGD
momentum	0.9
d_{model}	160
head	8
FFN size	480
Embed dropout	0.5
Output dropout	0.3
dh	100
warmup	10 (epoch)

4.2 Overall Performance

In this section, we compare our model with models listed below:

- TFIDF+SVM: TFIDF+SVM is a joint model that uses a bag of words model with TF-IDF for feature extraction and SVM as the classifier.
- FastText: FastText [20] is an efficient method for text classification that feeds the weighted average n-gram embeddings of the sentence into a linear function to obtain the final category.

- LEAM: LEAM [22] puts the embeddings of words and labels into a unified space for text classification. Among all the comparison methods, LEAM is tested in character-level and word-level, respectively.
- GCN: GCN [5] constructs the heterogeneous graph including word (or character) nodes and sentence nodes which are encoded via the GCN in the graph.
- CharCNN: CharCNN [25] applies the character-level CNN model for the text classification task.
- TextCNN: TextCNN [23] utilizes the pretrained word vectors for sentence embedding and uses a CNN layer for sentence-level classification.
- DPCNN: DPCNN [24] is a deep pyramid CNN architecture built on the word-level with strong representation ability.
- BLSTM-C: BLSTM-C [36] is a hybrid neural model consisting of a bidirectional LSTM layer and a CNN layer for Chinese text classification.
- HAN: The GRU based sequence encoder in HAN [24] uses the hierarchical attention mechanism for word-level document classification.
- Albert-tiny: Albert-tiny [31] that is the tiny version of the lite BERT is fine-tuned in the Chinese text classification task.
- Bi-Lattice: Bi-Lattice [37] utilizes the bidirectional lattice LSTM network for Chinese text classification.

Table 3. Comparison results on the two datasets.

Models	#Dataset 1				#Dataset 2			
	P	R	F1	ACC	P	R	F1	ACC
TFIDF+SVM	75.5	75.6	75.8	75.3	58.4	56.9	57.6	59.7
FastText	78.70	78.29	78.34	78.27	56.96	53.90	54.81	56.99
LEAM (char)	75.49	75.64	75.83	75.33	58.44	56.85	57.62	59.67
LEAM (word)	76.29	76.20	76.21	76.51	62.45	60.87	61.71	63.87
GCN (char)	74.77	74.56	74.55	74.54	55.95	53.81	54.57	58.28
GCN (word)	77.38	77.54	77.39	77.56	59.25	57.74	58.27	63.12
CharCNN	74.28	74.35	74.21	74.30	58.11	57.09	57.37	61.25
TextCNN	69.21	68.26	68.38	68.20	57.13	54.67	55.18	57.76
DPCNN	74.90	72.67	73.07	72.61	52.94	52.22	52.82	55.84
TextRNN	74.48	74.57	74.33	74.57	54.60	52.38	52.96	56.37
BLSTM-C	77.20	76.72	76.50	76.66	55.74	53.57	53.78	57.08
HAN	77.28	77.74	77.67	77.86	58.29	55.54	56.58	58.26
Albert-tiny	81.28	81.24	81.23	81.22	61.49	59.46	60.12	62.79
Bi-Lattice	82.31	82.21	82.13	82.17	62.64	61.00	61.65	63.62
Our model	**84.45**	**84.16**	**83.30**	**84.28**	**64.58**	**62.97**	**63.76**	**65.27**

Table 3 shows the comparison results of our proposed method with other baseline ones. From this table, we can draw the following conclusions: 1) Compared with shallow models such as TF-IDF+SVM, deep models can achieve better performance both in Dataset 1 and Dataset 2. The reason might be that deep models can better learn semantic information in the sentence; 2) The performance of models which are based on words is higher than those based on characters since words have better semantic expression; 3) The lattice model such as Bi-Lattice has higher performance in terms of all the evaluation metrics, which means that the lattice model has better capability for learning both of the character-level and word-level information; 4) Compared with all the baseline methods, our proposed method achieves the best performance, demonstrating that context information, character-level and word-level information are all important for Chinese text classification, and our model is good at leveraging these information.

5 Conclusion

In this paper, we propose a novel method for Chinese text classification which uses the flat-lattice transformer to integrate both of the character-level and word-level vector representation. To obtain character-level vector representation, we adopt the BERT model which has demonstrated to achieve good performance in most NLP tasks. While for word-level vector representation, we utilize word2vec to learn lexicon information. Extensive of experiments demonstrate the effectiveness of our proposed method and show superior performance over the baseline methods. Our future work will be committed to discovering different kinds of lattice or graph.

Acknowledgements. This paper is Supported in part by a grant from Guangxi Key Laboratory of Machine Vision and Intelligent Control, the Provincial College Students Innovation and Entrepreneurship Training Program Project (S202211354104). This work is also supported by the Shenzhen Development and Reform Commission subject (XMHT20200105010).

References

1. Chen, Y., Xu, L., Liu, K., Zeng, D.: Event extraction via dynamic multi-pooling convolutional neural networks. In: Proceedings of the 53rd Annual Meeting of the Association for Computational Linguistics and the 7th International Joint Conference on Natural Language Processing, pp. 167–176 (2015)
2. Diefenbach, D., Lopez, V.: Singh, K: Core techniques of question answering systems over knowledge bases: a survey. Knowl. Inf. Syst. **55**(3), 529–569 (2018)
3. Ren, F., Deng, J.: Background knowledge based multi-stream neural network for text classification. Appl. Sci. **8**(12), 2472 (2018)
4. Tao, H., Tong, S., Zhao, H., Xu, T., Jin, B., Liu, Q.: A radical-aware attention-based model for Chinese text classification. In: The Thirty-Third AAAI Conference on Artificial Intelligence (AAAI 2019), USA, 27 January–1 February 2019
5. Yao, L., Mao, C., Luo, Y.: Graph convolutional networks for text classification. In: Proceedings of the AAAI Conference on Artificial Intelligence, vol. 33, pp. 7370 7377 (2019)

6. Tian, J., Zhu, D., Long, H.: Chinese short text multi-classification based on word and part-of-speech tagging embedding. In: Proceedings of the 2018 International Conference on Algorithms, Computing and Artificial Intelligence, pp. 1–6 (2018)
7. Zhou, J., Lu, Y., Dai, H.N., Wang, H., Xiao, H.: Sentiment analysis of Chinese microblog based on stacked bidirectional LSTM. IEEE Access **7**, 38856–38866 (2019)
8. Zhou, Y., Xu, B., Xu, J., Yang, L., Li, C.: Compositional recurrent neural networks for Chinese short text classification. In: 2016 IEEE/WIC/ACM International Conference on Web Intelligence (WI), pp. 137–144. IEEE (2016)
9. Zhang, Y., Yang, J.: Chinese NER using lattice LSTM. arXiv preprint arXiv:1805.02023 (2018)
10. Zhao, H., Huang, C., Li, M.: An improved Chinese word segmentation system with conditional random field. In: Proceedings of the Fifth SIGHAN Workshop on Chinese Language Processing, Sydney, pp. 162–165 (2006)
11. Gui, T., Ma, R., Zhang, Q., Zhao, L., et al.: CNN- based Chinese NER with lexicon rethinking. In: Proceedings of the 28th International Joint Conference on Artificial Intelligence, IJCAI 2019, pp. 4982–4988. AAAI Press (2019)
12. Gui, T., Zou, Y., Zhang, Q., et al.: A lexicon-based graph neural network for Chinese NER. In Proceedings of the 2019 Conference on Empirical Methods in Natural Language Processing and the 9th International Joint Conference on Natural Language Processing (EMNLP-IJCNLP), Hong Kong, China, pp. 1039–1049. Association for Computational Linguistics (2019)
13. Sui, D., Chen, Y., Liu, K., Zhao, J., Liu, S.: Leverage lexical knowledge for Chinese named entity recognition via collaborative graph network. In Proceedings of the 2019 Conference on Empirical Methods in Natural Language Processing and the 9th International Joint Conference on Natural Language Processing (EMNLPIJCNLP), pp. 3821–3831. Association for Computational Linguistics, Hong Kong, China (2019)
14. Li, X., Yan, H., Qiu, X., Huang, X.: FLAT: Chinese NER using flat-lattice transformer. arXiv preprint arXiv:2004.11795 (2020)
15. Lee, J. D. M. C. K., Toutanova, K.: BERT: pre-training of deep bidirectional transformers for language understanding. arXiv preprint arXiv:1810.04805 (2018)
16. Vaswani, A., Shazeer, N., Parmar, N., et al.: Attention is all you need. In: Guyon, I., et al. (eds.) Advances in Neural Information Processing Systems 30, pp. 5998–6008. Curran Associates, Inc. (2017)
17. Goudjil, M., Koudil, M., Bedda, M., Ghoggali, N.: A novel active learning method using SVM for text classification. Int. J. Autom. Comput. **15**(3), 290–298 (2018)
18. Blei, D.M., Ng, A.Y., Jordan, M.I.: Latent Dirichlet allocation. J. Mach. Learn. Res. **3**, 993–1022 (2003)
19. Mikolov, T., Sutskever, I., Chen, K., Corrado, G.S., Dean, J.: Distributed representations of words and phrases and their compositionality. In: Advances in Neural Information Processing Systems, pp. 3111–3119 (2013)
20. Joulin, A., Grave, E., Bojanowski, P., Mikolov, T.: Bag of tricks for efficient text classification. arXiv preprint arXiv:1607.01759 (2016)
21. Le, Q., Mikolov, T.: Distributed representations of sentences and documents. In: International Conference on Machine Learning, pp. 1188–1196 (2014)
22. Wang, G., Li, C., et al.: Joint embedding of words and labels for text classification. arXiv preprint arXiv:1805.04174 (2018)
23. Kim, Y.: Convolutional neural networks for sentence classification. arXiv preprint arXiv: 1408.5882 (2014)
24. Johnson, R., Zhang, T.: Deep pyramid convolutional neural networks for text categorization. In: Proceedings of the 55th Annual Meeting of the Association for Computational Linguistics (ACL 2017) Volume 1: Long Papers, Vancouver, Canada, 30 July–4 August 2017 (2017)

25. Zhang, X., Zhao, J., LeCun, Y.: Character-level convolutional networks for text classification. In: Advances in Neural Information Processing Systems, pp. 649–657 (2015)
26. Luo, Y.: Recurrent neural networks for classifying relations in clinical notes. J. Biomed. Inform. **72**, 85–95 (2017)
27. Tai, K.S., Socher, R., Manning, C.D.: Improved semantic representations from tree-structured long short-term memory networks. In: Proceedings of the 53rd Annual Meeting of the Association for Computational Linguistics (ACL 2015) Volume 1: Long Papers, Beijing, China, 26–31 July 2015 (2015)
28. Yang, Z., Yang, D., Dyer, C., He, X., Smola, A., Hovy, E.: Hierarchical attention networks for document classification. In: Proceedings of the 2016 Conference of the North American Chapter of the Association for Computational Linguistics: Human Language Technologies, pp. 1480–1489 (2016)
29. Yao, L., Mao, C., Luo, Y.: Graph convolutional networks for text classification. In: Proceedings of the AAAI Conference on Artificial Intelligence, vol. 33, no. 01, pp. 7370–7377 (2019)
30. Sabour, S., Frosst, N., Hinton, G.E.: Dynamic routing between capsules. In: Advances in Neural Information Processing Systems, pp. 3856–3866 (2017)
31. Lan, Z., Chen, M., Goodman, S., Gimpel, K., Sharma, P., Soricut, R.: ALBERT: a lite BERT for self-supervised learning of language representations. arXiv preprint arXiv:1909.11942 (2019)
32. Yang, Z., Dai, Z., Yang, Y., Carbonell, J.G., Salakhutdinov, R., Le, Q.V.: XLNet: generalized autoregressive pretraining for language understanding. In: Advances in Neural Information Processing Systems 32: Annual Conference on Neural Information Processing Systems 2019, NeurIPS 2019, Vancouver, BC, Canada, 8–14 December 2019 (2019)
33. Yang, J., Zhang, Y., Liang, S.: Subword encoding in lattice LSTM for Chinese word segmentation. arXiv preprint arXiv:1810.12594 (2018)
34. Yan, H., Deng, B., Li, X., Qiu, X.: TENER: adapting transformer encoder for named entity recognition. arXiv preprint arXiv:1911.04474 (2019)
35. Dai, Z., Yang, Z., Yang, Y., et al.: Transformer-XL: attentive language models beyond a fixed-length context. arXiv preprint arXiv:1901.02860 (2019)
36. Li, Y., Wang, X., Xu, P.: Chinese text classification model based on deep learning. Future Internet **10**(11), 113 (2018)
37. Cui, Y., Che, W., Liu, T., et al.: Pre-training with whole word masking for Chinese BERT. IEEE/ACM Trans. Audio Speech Lang. Process. **29**, 3504–3514 (2021)
38. Pang, N., Xiao, W., Zhao, X.: Chinese text classification via bidirectional lattice LSTM. In: Li, G., Shen, H.T., Yuan, Ye., Wang, X., Liu, H., Zhao, X. (eds.) KSEM 2020. LNCS (LNAI), vol. 12275, pp. 250–262. Springer, Cham (2020). https://doi.org/10.1007/978-3-030-55393-7_23

Indicator-Specific Recurrent Neural Networks with Co-teaching for Stock Trend Prediction

Hongling Xu[1,3], Jingqian Zhao[1,3], Xiaoqi Yu[2,3], Yixue Dang[2,3], Yang Sun[1,3], Jianzhu Bao[1,3], and Ruifeng Xu[1,3(✉)]

[1] School of Computer Science and Technology,
Harbin Institute of Technology (Shenzhen), Shenzhen, China
`sy95@mail.ustc.edu.cn, xuruifeng@hit.edu.cn`
[2] China Merchants Securities Co., Ltd., Shenzhen, China
`{yuxiaoqi,dangyixue}@cmschina.com.cn`
[3] Joint Lab of HITSZ-CMS, Shenzhen, China

Abstract. Stock trend prediction is a challenging problem due to the complexity of stock data. Recently, many works applied deep learning methods for stock trend prediction and achieve impressive results. However, these methods still suffer from two limitations: 1) Various types of technical indicators are input into a single model, making it difficult for the model to learn differentiated features. 2) Noisy data in the stocks is not handled effectively. Therefore, in this paper, we propose a stock trend prediction framework using indicator-specific recurrent neural networks with co-teaching. Specifically, we first collect data from Chinese stock market and divide them into fourteen categories. Then we apply multiple RNNs to extract features separately from different technical indicator categories which can learn comprehensive features. In addition, we leverage multi-head attention for effective feature interaction and fusion. At last, we utilize co-teaching method during the training process to reduce the impact of noisy data. Experimental results show both the effectiveness and superiority of our method.

Keywords: RNN · Attention mechanism · Co-teaching · Stock prediction

1 Introduction

As an important part of economic research, predicting stock trends have received many interests in recent years, which is of great significance to economic development, social progress as well as individual investors [10,22,35].

However, whether the trends of stock can be predicted remains a controversial topic, because it is influenced by a variety of sophisticated factors, such as social issues, public sentiment, political events, etc. On the one hand, [11] propose the famous "Efficient Capital Markets" theory, which is further deepened into Efficient Markets Hypothesis (EMH). According to the EMH, important information can be disseminated very quickly and affect stock prices immediately. If a method of predicting stock prices is made public, then it can quickly affect the stock market and lead to stock price fluctuations [22,25]. Therefore, it is very difficult to predict the market continuously. On the other hand, The EMH is related to the concept of "random walk", a financial term used to describe the random deviation of all subsequent price changes from the previous price [26]. The random walk theory on stock market indicates that the correlation for day-to-day stock price changes is very low [14,27]. Thus it negates the possibility of using past prices to predict today's prices.

So far there is no consensus on the feasibility of stock prediction. Many researchers from different fields have been trying to achieve a practical stock prediction model, and have proposed a large variety of methods. These methods could be broadly divided into three categories: traditional methods [5,28], machine learning-based methods [2,16,31], deep learning-based methods [6,18,29,30].

Although significant performance gains can be achieved using deep learning-based methods, there are still some shortcomings. First, due to the complexity and diversity characteristics of stock features [1], most previous work establishes an integral model for feature extraction or interaction and uses multiple indicators for prediction [7,8,18]. However, if the features of several indicators differ significantly from each other, it is likely to cause information loss during the interaction, which in turn suppresses the model performance. Second, most approaches use sequential models, such as recurrent neural networks (RNNs) for global information modeling, which suffer from the long-term dependency and poor parallelism issues [18,23,29]. Third, the existence of noisy data is common in stock trend prediction tasks [4,12], which has rarely been considered in past methods.

To tackle the above issues, we propose a framework using multi-RNNs and feature-based attention mechanism for stock trend prediction. Specifically, since the technical indicators we use can be grouped into different categories, we train a RNN for each category as its sequential feature extractor. In this way, if the features of several indicator categories differ a lot from each other, more differentiated features can be learned by multiple RNNs, thus the information loss will be reduced. In addition, we adopt multi-head attention with learnable query for global feature interaction, in which various kinds of features are aggregated with different weights through the attention mechanism. Further, to alleviate the negative effects caused by noisy data, we adopt JoCoR to train two networks simultaneously [33], which uses samples with higher reliability to update parameters and co-regularization to increase the similarity between models. This strategy can mitigate the effects of noisy data and improve the generalization ability of our model by making the two models learn similar high-confidence samples.

Our contribution can be summarized as follows:

- We collect various stock data from the Chinese stock market, and categorize them into 14 kinds of technical indicators based on different analytical characteristics.

– We propose to train an independent RNN model as the feature extractor
  for each category of indicators to reduce information loss, and use attention
  mechanism for feature aggregation.
– We utilize the co-teaching method to deal with the noisy data, which can
  effectively enhance the performance of our model.
– Experiments results show that our model significantly outperforms all the
  baseline methods, which demonstrates the superiority of our approach.

2 Related Work

2.1 Technical Indicators

Technical indicators are time series statistics generated by analyzing market
activities, such as past prices, trends and volume, which are the most commonly used solutions for stock trend prediction. Moving Average (MA) is one
of the most widely used technical indicators, which describes the average stock
price in a predefined time window. Based on the assumption of different importance at different time points, it can be classified into simple moving average
(SMA), weighted moving average (WMA), exponential moving average (EMA)
and so on [8]. Another commonly used type of technical indicator is the oscilla-
tor, including moving average convergence divergence (MACD), relative strength
index (RSI) and others. Among these, moving average convergence/divergence
(MACD) describes the difference between two EMAs while relative strength
index (RSI) compares the magnitude of a stock's recent gains to the magnitude
of its recent losses [1].

2.2 Stock Trend Prediction Model

Early methods applied time series models such as auto-regressive models (ARM)
and moving average models for stock prediction. For example, [5] apply four
auto-regressive models to design trading strategies and test them on Dow Jones
index, which is a commonly used index that reflects overall U.S. trading market
conditions.

   However, stock data contains a large number of complex features, which
are difficult to model with the linear models. There are several works introduced machine learning methods for dealing with non-linear feature interactions. [19,34] put forward using artificial neural networks (ANN) for economic
prediction. [16,31] apply support vector machine (SVM) to forecast stock market direction. [17] compared the performance of SVM with ANN on stock index
movement prediction. [3] introduce extensive process on stock price prediction
via leveraging auto-regressive integrated moving average (ARIMA) models. [37]
propose a hybrid approach, using AdaBoost algorithm to improve the performance of SVM and genetic algorithm (GA) to optimize the parameters. [21]
conduct a comprehensive study to compare several machine learning methods
for stock trend prediciotn, including SVM, Random Forest, k-nearest neighbor
(KNN), naive bayes and so on.

Although the above methods have achieved promising progress, they still need manually designed features, and is difficult to extract high-level representations of input features. With the development of deep learning models, time series prediction have been proved to achieve better performance with convolutional neural networks (CNN) or recurrent neural networks (RNN). [29] designed a RNN-based hybrid stock prediction model, which utilizes RNN with autoregressive moving reference and GA is used to optimize. As a variant of RNN that can mitigate gradient problem, Long short-term Memory (LSTM) is also widely used for this task. [27] proposed using stock price and some technical indicators to train a LSTM model for trend prediction. Furthermore, [18] put forward leveraging LSTM along with attention mechanism for financial series prediction, where attention mechanism are used both on time and factors, and LSTM networks are stacked for learning deeper stock feature representation. [15] proposed a CNN-based neural network which can be applied on different markets. [23] introduced a CNN-LSTM-Attention framework to extract stock feature and use attention mechanism to calculate weighted summation over time steps for stock price prediction.

In this work, we propose using multi-RNNs and feature-based attention for stock trend prediction. Different from previous methods, we apply multiple RNNs to extract features from different kinds of technical indicators. In addition, our feature-based attention mechanism is designed for different indicators to capture the interaction and aggregation representations of them.

2.3   Co-teaching for Noisy Data

Noisy labels have been proved to affect the performance of the deep neural networks [1]. To address this problem, some co-teaching methods have been proposed, which means to select some of the predictions from two models to update parameters. [24] first put forward training two models, and use decoupling strategy which means updating parameters only in case of disagreement between two models. In Co-teaching [13], both models back propagate with small-loss instances selected by each other. Improving on the above foundation, [36] introduce Co-teaching+ combining with decoupling strategy and co-teaching strategy to enhance the robustness of the models. To better handle the memorization effects on noisy labels, JoCoR (Joint Training with Co-Regularization) is proposed [33]. Specifically, two models are trained with a joint loss, including traditional supervised training loss and co-regularization loss. During the training process, samples with small joint loss are selected for updating the parameters. To the best of our knowledge, Co-teaching methods have rarely been applied to deal with stock trend prediction challenge.

3   Dataset

3.1   Data Acquisition

We construct the stock trend prediction dataset based on the stock data provided by China Merchants Securities. The stock data provides technical indicators in

Table 1. The feature descriptions of the 14 tables.

Name	Description
AF	Reflects the analyst on the trend forecast of individual stocks
CF	Reflects the company's cash flow information
DERIVE	Derivative of financial report data
GROWTH	Reflects the company's growth, such as net profit growth rate
MA	The average index of stock prices
OBOS	Overbuying of a stock is called overbought, and overselling of a stock is called oversold
OC	Reflects the company's operating status or operating level
POWER	Measure whether stock sentiment is high or depressed
PQ	Reflects the company's profitability and earnings
PSI	Fundamental information related to each share
RETURN	Factors related to earnings, reflecting the correlation between earnings and the broader market
SC	Reflects whether the company's ability to repay debt
TREND	Measure of stock trend
VS	Reflects the market to the company's valuation size and some market value related factors

tabular units and there are 14 tabular data. Each tabular data represents a class of characteristics of stocks, and Table 1 shows the feature descriptions of the 14 tables.

3.2 Data Processing

The stock data contains four types of features: continuous type features, discrete type features, continuous time series type features and discrete time series type features. When processing the data, we first evaluate the availability of each technical indicators, and filter out the indicators that have serious miss values or have no significance for the trend prediction. After that, we perform missing value filling, continuous feature normalization, discrete feature coding, temporal feature normalization, time interception, frequency alignment, and so on. For the filling of missing values, we divided it into two steps: The data is first grouped by stock, and then propagated forward through time to fill in the missing values. For the remaining missing values, we group stocks by date and fill them with the mean of all stocks on the same day.

Table 2. Dataset description

	Training	Testing	Sum
Positive	48138	20730	68868
Negative	48765	20730	69495

3.3 Dataset Construction

We collected and processed nearly three years of stock data with N processed tables of technical indicator, we construct the stock trend prediction dataset via setting historical time window size to M (M = 30 in this paper) and forecasting time window size to n (n = 30 in this paper). Specifically, for each sample, we select a time anchor point, the time series features $X = \{x_1, x_2, \ldots, x_M\}$ in the past m days (including the time anchor point) with N indicator categories as the input features. The trend label $y \in \{positive, negative\}$ in the next n days can be labelled by the comparison between the price of the time anchor point and the price of the last day in the next n day. In each time step of the time series features X, the feature x_i consists of N indicator categories $\{p_1, p_2, \ldots, p_N\}$, the number of the technical indicators in the i-th categories are k_i. Table 2 shows the details of the constructed dataset.

4 Methodology

4.1 Task Definition

Given a sample $X = \{x_1, x_2, \ldots, x_M\}$ in the past m days with N features, our goal is to predict the trend label $y \in \{positive, negative\}$ in the next n days. In each time step of the time series features X, the feature x_i consists of N indicator categories $\{p_1, p_2, \ldots, p_N\}$, the number of the technical indicators in the i-th categories are k_i.

4.2 Model Overview

Figure 1 shows the overall architecture of the proposed model. Our model consists of 3 modules: 1) *feature extraction module*, which contains multiple RNNs to extract representations from different kinds of technical indicators. RNN model converts time series data of each indicator into higher-level feature representation. 2) *feature-based attention module*, which leverages Multi-Head Attention for global feature interaction by calculating the weighted summation of indicator representations. 3) *prediction module*, which feeds the attention output results into MLP followed by a softmax layer for trend prediction.

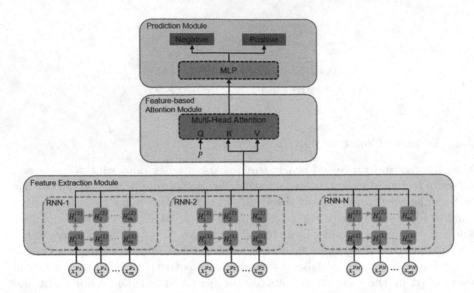

Fig. 1. Model overview.

4.3 Feature Extraction Module

Since the technical indicators within different indicators categories represent different characteristics of stocks, we use different RNNs to model each category of indicators as a sequence feature extractor. Each RNN can independently learn the representations of a class of technical indicators.

Each sample contains N indicator categories, and the number of the technical indicators in the i-th category is k_i. We divide X into N sequences as $\{X^{p_1}, X^{p_2}, \ldots, X^{p_N}\}$, where $X^{p_i} = \{x_1^{p_i}, x_2^{p_i}, \ldots, x_m^{p_i}\}$ in the category p_i and $x_m^{p_i} \in \mathbb{R}^{k_i}$ and $1 \leq m \leq M$. For each feature sequence of each indicator category, we utilize a RNN as the feature extractor where the hidden size is set to d.

Take the i-th RNN feature extractor as a example, the values of the hidden units at the l-th layer $H_t^{(l)} \in \mathbb{R}^{m \times d}$ are defined as follows:

$$H_t^{(l)} = tanh(H_t^{(l-1)}W_{ih}^{(l)} + H_{t-1}^{(l)}W_{hh}^{(l)} + b_h^{(l)}) \qquad (1)$$

where $H_0^1 = x_t^{p_i}$. $W_{ih}^{(1)} \in \mathbb{R}^{k_i \times d}$, $W_{ih}^{(2)} \in \mathbb{R}^{d \times d}$ and $W_{hh}^{(l)} \in \mathbb{R}^{d \times d}$ are the weight matrices, $b_h^{(1)} \in \mathbb{R}^{1 \times d}$ is the bias term, and $tanh$ is the activation function. After that, we can obtain the flattened representations $H_i \in \mathbb{R}^{1 \times md}$ of the i-th indicator category.

4.4 Feature-Based Attention Module

Because different indicator categories may have different importance for stock trend prediction. We apply attention mechanism to interact with different types of technical indicators, and assign higher weights to technical indicators that can contribute more to stock trend prediction.

Given a learnable parameter $P \in \mathbb{R}^{1 \times md}$ as the query, the i-th indicator category representations H_i as the key and value, we leverage Scaled Dot-Production Attention scoring function $att(\cdot)$: $\mathbb{R}^d \times \mathbb{R}^d \rightarrow \mathbb{R}$ to compute the attention coefficient β_i denoting the importance score of indicator category i for trend prediction:

$$\beta_i = att(\mathbf{W}^Q P, \mathbf{W}^K H_i) = \frac{[W^Q P][W^K H_i]^T}{\sqrt{d_k}} \tag{2}$$

where H_i is the representation of i-th indicator category, $W_i^Q \in \mathbb{R}^{d_k \times md}, W_i^K \in \mathbb{R}^{d_k \times md}$ are learnable parameters. To make the coefficients easily comparable across different indicator categories, we normalize β_i across all choices of i with softmax:

$$\hat{\beta}_i = softmax(\beta_i) = \frac{exp(\beta_i)}{\sum_{j=1}^N exp(\beta_j)} \tag{3}$$

After that, we calculate a global representation $\mathbf{Z}$ by using the weighted sum over H^i as follows, where $W_i^V \in \mathbb{R}^{d_k \times md}$ is learnable parameters:

$$\mathbf{Z} = \sum_{i=1}^N \hat{\beta}_i W^V H_i \tag{4}$$

To stabilize the learning process of attention mechanism, we have found employing multi-head attention [32] is more beneficial. Specifically, K independent attention mechanism execute the transformation of Eq. (4), and then their features are concatenated, resulting in the following output feature representation:

$$\mathbf{Z} = W^O [\bigcap_{k=1}^K (\sum_{i=1}^N \hat{\beta}_i^k W_k^V H_i)]^T \tag{5}$$

where $\bigcap$ represents concatenation operation, $\hat{\beta}_i^k$ are normalized attention coefficients computed by the k-th attention head. $W_k^V \in \mathbb{R}^{d_k \times md}$ and $W^O \in \mathbb{R}^{md \times md}$ are learnable parameters, and $\mathbf{Z} \in \mathbb{R}^{md \times 1}$ is the output of the attention module.

4.5 Prediction Module

After deriving the output $\mathbf{Z}$ from the multi-head attention, the aggregated feature representation is fed into a multi-layer perceptron (MLP) and a softmax classifier to calculate the probabilities distribution $p(\hat{y})$ of predicted trend labels as follows:

$$p(\hat{y} \mid x) = softmax(W_2 \cdot RELU(W_1 \cdot \mathbf{Z} + b_1) + b_2) \tag{6}$$

where $W_1 \in \mathbb{R}^{md \times h}, W_2 \in \mathbb{R}^{h \times 2}$ are the weight matrix, and $b_1 \in \mathbb{R}^{1 \times h}, b_2 \in \mathbb{R}^{h \times 2}$ are the bias terms, and $RELU$ is the ReLU function.

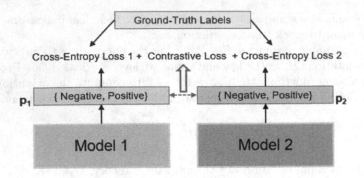

Fig. 2. Illustration of joint loss for co-teaching.

4.6 Co-teaching

Due to stock data containing a large number of noise, which cause the problem of noisy labels. Inspired by [33], we apply co-teaching method to reduce the impact of noisy labels, and improve the robustness and generalization of our model. Specifically, we employ two models with the same architecture but different initialization, which are denoted as $f(D, \Theta_1)$ and $f(D, \Theta_2)$ where D is the set of all training samples. We denote $p_1 = [p_1^{pos}, p_1^{neg}]$ and $p_2 = [p_2^{pos}, p_2^{neg}]$ as the prediction probabilities of the two models for instance X respectively.

To encourage model learn the true label, we apply the agreement maximization principle to tackle the problem of noisy labels. That is, we steer two different classifiers to make predictions closer to each other by explicit regularization method. This method could by considered as a meta-algorithm that trains two base classifiers by one loss function, which includes a regularization term to reduce divergence between the two classifiers.

As Fig. 2 shows, during the training stage the two models can be updated simultaneously by a joint loss, which includes the cross-entropy loss and a contrastive term as Co-regularization to reduce divergence between the two models. To measure the match of two models predictions, we adopt the Jensen-Shannon(JS) Divergence, and to simplify implementation, we use the symmetric Kullback-Leibler(KL) Divergence to surrogate the contrastive term. The loss function consists of two parts as follows:

$$\ell_{ce}(D) = \ell_{CE1}(D) + \ell_{CE2}(D)$$
$$= -\frac{1}{|D|} \left(\sum_{(X,y) \in D} y \log(p_1) + \sum_{(X,y) \in D} y \log(p_2) \right) \tag{7}$$

$$\ell_c(D) = D_{KL}(p_1 \| p_2) + D_{KL}(p_2 \| p_1)$$

$$= \sum_{(X,y) \in D} (p_1^{pos}(X) \log \frac{p_1^{pos}(X)}{p_2^{pos}(X)} + p_1^{neg}(X) \log \frac{p_1^{neg}(X)}{p_2^{neg}(X)})$$

$$+ \sum_{(X,y) \in D} (p_2^{pos}(X) \log \frac{p_2^{pos}(X)}{p_1^{pos}(X)} + p_2^{neg}(X) \log \frac{p_2^{neg}(X)}{p_1^{neg}(X)}) \tag{8}$$

Finally, we combine the cross-entropy loss $\ell_{ce}(D)$ for stock trend prediction with the contrastive loss $\ell_c(D)$ for co-teaching between predictions of the two model as the objective loss:

$$\ell(D) = (1 - \lambda) * \ell_{ce}(D) + \lambda * \ell_c(D) \tag{9}$$

5 Experiment

5.1 Experimental Setting

We use PyTorch to implement the proposed framework on a Nvidia Tesla V100 GPU. Our model is optimized using Adam [20] with the learning rates of 5e−5. We set the epoch and batch size to 20 and 128. In feature extraction module, RNN hidden dimension d is 384 and the number of layers l is 2. In feature-based attention module, head number is set to 16. We randomly divide the dataset into a training set and a test set in the ratio of 7:3. Following most of the previous work [8,9], the metrics we use are Accuracy and F1-score. The F_1 score is computed by considering true positives (TP), false positives (FP) and false negatives (FN) as $F_1 = \frac{2TP}{2TP + FP + FN}$. Moreover, we conduct the significance t-test to demonstrate that the effect of our model is significantly better than the baseline models.

5.2 Results and Analysis

Baseline Methods. To demonstrate the performance of the proposed model, we develop the following methods including machine learning methods and deep learning models as the baselines for comparison.

Logistic Regression uses all kinds of indicator features to train a linear classifier.

XGBoost apply a XGBoost classifier for trend prediction with all indicator features.

SVM employ a SVM to encoder all indicator features.

Multi-RNNs + MLP has only one feature extractor for all indicator categories and uses a MLP to encoder the indicator representations.

Multi-CNNs + MLP uses N Text-CNNs for feature extraction. and the extracted features are concatenated as input of a MLP for stock trend prediction

Table 3. Main experiment results. The best results are in bold. (%)

Model	ACC	F1
Machine learning methods		
Logistic Regression	64.15	61.01
XGBoost	64.64	61.17
SVM	65.10	60.37
Deep learning methods		
Multi-CNNs + MLP	67.64	66.93
Multi-RNNs + MLP	69.73	68.40
Our Model	**70.92**†	**70.45**†

Main Results. Table 3 shows the main experimental results, from which the following conclusions can be drawn. 1) Our model significantly outperforms all baselines, which demonstrates the effectiveness of our model. 2) In machine learning algorithms, the stacked model XGBOOST or a non-linear model SVM would be better than the simple linear classifier, which represents the machine learning models can model complex non-linear features for stock trend prediction. 3) The deep learning approach significantly outperforms the simple machine learning classifier, indicating that the deep learning approach is effective to model high-level representations for stock data. 4) The use of RNN as a feature extractor significantly outperforms the effect of CNN, showing that RNN is more conducive to process time-series data of stocks technical indicators than CNN. 5) $\dagger$ shows that the performance of our model is significantly better than the baseline models with $p\text{-}value < 0.05$ based on t-test.

5.3 Ablation Study

To demonstrate the effectiveness of each component in our model, We conduct ablation studied for four components of our model: 1) "w/o co-teaching" denotes the removal of the co-teaching strategy during training. 2) "w/o attention" means replacing the feature-based attention module with a simple average pooling layer to obtain global representation. 3) "w/o attention and co-teaching" removes the feature-based attention module strategy on top of "pooling". 4) "w/o multi-layer" means extracting features by single-layer RNNs instead of 2-layer. 5) "w/o multi-RNN" utilizes a single RNN to extract all kinds of features instead of multiple extractors.

Table 4 shows the ablation results. We find that "w/o co-teaching" achieves worse performance, which drops 0.67% accuracy and 0.69% F1 score, respectively. This is because the co-teaching strategy can alleviate the noise label problem by mutually feed samples with higher reliability into each other for the two models. We also observe that "w/o attention" and "w/o attention and co-teaching" also decreases the performance, which means attention mechanism

Table 4. Ablation experiment results. The best results are in bold. (%)

Model	ACC	F1
Model (w/o co-teaching)	70.25	69.76
Model (w/o attention)	69.94	69.49
Model (w/o attention and co-teaching)	70.06	68.99
Model (w/o multi-layer)	70.44	70.03
Model (w/o multi-RNN)	70.32	69.62
Our model	**70.92**	**70.45**

is important for feature aggregation by aligning different weights to different indicators. Besides, "w/o multi-layer" causes some performance degradation as well, indicating that more hidden layers can learn more non-linear information. In addition, The accuracy and $F1$ score decreases by 0.6% and 0.83%, respectively when using only a single RNN to extract all kinds of indicators with time series type feature. It implies that the independence among indicators in different tables and the our model acquire indicator-specific representations from different indicator categories by multi-RNNs module.

5.4 Case Study

To explore the correlation between the features from different indicators categories, we conduct case study to visualize the correlation heat map by calculating the similarity among different indicator features in Fig. 4. Specifically, we first randomly select a sample which the model predict correctly from the test dataset. Then, we obtain the features of the 14 tables extracted from the sample and calculate the correlation coefficients by Pearson product-moment correlation coefficient. We can observe that the similarity among different indicator is always small (<0.15). Furthermore, we show the attention weights in the feature-based attention module, which are calculated by taking the features of each table as key with the query learned in the training process. Different indicator categories have different contribution to the final prediction result. For this sample, The

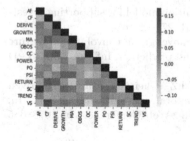

Fig. 3. Correlation matrix

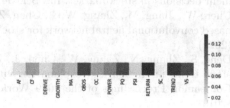

Fig. 4. Attention weights

OBOS, PQ, RETURN, TREND and V5 have bigger attention weights, which are above 0.1 (Fig. 3).

6 Conclusion

In this paper, we propose a new stock trend prediction model. In particular, to acquire indicator-specific representation, we train multiple RNNs to extract features from different categories of technical indicators. Then we apply the multi-head attention mechanism to capture the relationships among different indicator categories. Moreover, we utilize the co-teaching strategy to alleviate noisy labels problem during training, which improves the robustness and generalization of our model. Experimental results show that our proposed method outperforms baselines, and ablation study demonstrates the effectiveness of each component in our model.

Acknowledgments. This work was partially supported by the National Natural Science Foundation of China (62006062, 62176076), Shenzhen Foundational Research Funding JCYJ20200109113441941, Shenzhen Key Technology Project JSGG20210802154400001 and Joint Lab of HITSZ and China Merchants Securities.

References

1. Agrawal, J., Chourasia, V., Mittra, A.: State-of-the-art in stock prediction techniques. Int. J. Adv. Res. Electr. Electron. Instrum. Eng. **2**(4), 1360–1366 (2013)
2. Ahmed, N.K., Atiya, A.F., Gayar, N.E., El-Shishiny, H.: An empirical comparison of machine learning models for time series forecasting. Econom. Rev. **29**(5–6), 594–621 (2010)
3. Ariyo, A.A., Adewumi, A.O., Ayo, C.K.: Stock price prediction using the ARIMA model. In: 2014 UKSim-AMSS 16th International Conference on Computer Modelling and Simulation, pp. 106–112. IEEE (2014)
4. Black, F.: Noise. J. Financ. **41**(3), 528–543 (1986)
5. Brock, W., Lakonishok, J., LeBaron, B.: Simple technical trading rules and the stochastic properties of stock returns. J. Financ. **47**(5), 1731–1764 (1992)
6. Chen, K., Zhou, Y., Dai, F.: A LSTM-based method for stock returns prediction: a case study of China stock market. In: 2015 IEEE International Conference on Big Data (Big Data), pp. 2823–2824. IEEE (2015)
7. Chen, T., Chen, F.: An intelligent pattern recognition model for supporting investment decisions in stock market. Inf. Sci. **346**, 261–274 (2016)
8. Chen, W., Jiang, M., Zhang, W.G., Chen, Z.: A novel graph convolutional feature based convolutional neural network for stock trend prediction. Inf. Sci. **556**, 67–94 (2021)
9. Deng, S., Zhang, N., Zhang, W., Chen, J., Pan, J.Z., Chen, H.: Knowledge-driven stock trend prediction and explanation via temporal convolutional network. In: Companion Proceedings of the 2019 World Wide Web Conference, pp. 678–685 (2019)
10. Egeli, B., Ozturan, M., Badur, B.: Stock market prediction using artificial neural networks. Decis. Support Syst. **22**, 171–185 (2003)

11. Fama, E.F.: Efficient capital markets: a review of theory and empirical work. J. Financ. **25**(2), 383–417 (1970)
12. Fenghua, W., Jihong, X., Zhifang, H., Xu, G.: Stock price prediction based on SSA and SVM. Procedia Comput. Sci. **31**, 625–631 (2014)
13. Han, B., et al.: Co-teaching: robust training of deep neural networks with extremely noisy labels. In: Advances in Neural Information Processing Systems 31 (2018)
14. Hellström, T., Holmström, K.: Predicting the stock market (1998)
15. Hoseinzade, E., Haratizadeh, S.: CNNpred: CNN-based stock market prediction using a diverse set of variables. Expert Syst. Appl. **129**, 273–285 (2019)
16. Huang, W., Nakamori, Y., Wang, S.Y.: Forecasting stock market movement direction with support vector machine. Compute. Oper. Res. **32**(10), 2513–2522 (2005)
17. Kara, Y., Boyacioglu, M.A., Baykan, Ö.K.: Predicting direction of stock price index movement using artificial neural networks and support vector machines: the sample of the Istanbul stock exchange. Expert Syst. Appl. **38**(5), 5311–5319 (2011)
18. Kim, S., Kang, M.: Financial series prediction using attention LSTM. arXiv preprint arXiv:1902.10877 (2019)
19. Kimoto, T., Asakawa, K., Yoda, M., Takeoka, M.: Stock market prediction system with modular neural networks. In: 1990 IJCNN International Joint Conference on Neural Networks, pp. 1–6. IEEE (1990)
20. Kingma, D.P., Ba, J.: Adam: a method for stochastic optimization. arXiv preprint arXiv:1412.6980 (2014)
21. Kumar, I., Dogra, K., Utreja, C., Yadav, P.: A comparative study of supervised machine learning algorithms for stock market trend prediction. In: 2018 Second International Conference on Inventive Communication and Computational Technologies (ICICCT), pp. 1003–1007. IEEE (2018)
22. Lawrence, R.: Using neural networks to forecast stock market prices. University of Manitoba, vol. 333, pp. 2006–2013 (1997)
23. Lu, W., Li, J., Wang, J., Qin, L.: A CNN-BILSTM-AM method for stock price prediction. Neural Comput. Appl. **33**(10), 4741–4753 (2021)
24. Malach, E., Shalev-Shwartz, S.: Decoupling "when to update" from "how to update". In: Advances in Neural Information Processing Systems 30 (2017)
25. Malkiel, B.G.: The efficient market hypothesis and its critics. J. Econ. Perspect. **17**(1), 59–82 (2003)
26. Malkiel, B.G.: A Random Walk Down Wall Street: Including a Life-Cycle Guide to Personal Investing. WW Norton & Company, New York (1999)
27. Nelson, D.M., Pereira, A.C., De Oliveira, R.A.: Stock market's price movement prediction with LSTM neural networks. In: 2017 International Joint Conference on Neural Networks (IJCNN), pp. 1419–1426. IEEE (2017)
28. Ou, J.A., Penman, S.H.: Financial statement analysis and the prediction of stock returns. J. Account. Econ. **11**(4), 295–329 (1989)
29. Rather, A.M., Agarwal, A., Sastry, V.: Recurrent neural network and a hybrid model for prediction of stock returns. Expert Syst. Appl. **42**(6), 3234–3241 (2015)
30. Saad, E.W., Prokhorov, D.V., Wunsch, D.C.: Comparative study of stock trend prediction using time delay, recurrent and probabilistic neural networks. IEEE Trans. Neural Netw. **9**(6), 1456–1470 (1998)
31. Trafalis, T.B., Ince, H.: Support vector machine for regression and applications to financial forecasting. In: Proceedings of the IEEE-INNS-ENNS International Joint Conference on Neural Networks. IJCNN 2000. Neural Computing: New Challenges and Perspectives for the New Millennium, vol. 6, pp. 348–353. IEEE (2000)
32. Vaswani, A., et al.: Attention is all you need. In: Advances in Neural Information Processing Systems 30 (2017)

33. Wei, H., Feng, L., Chen, X., An, B.: Combating noisy labels by agreement: a joint training method with co-regularization. In: Proceedings of the IEEE/CVF Conference on Computer Vision and Pattern Recognition, pp. 13726–13735 (2020)
34. White, H.: Economic prediction using neural networks: the case of IBM daily stock returns. In: ICNN, vol. 2, pp. 451–458 (1988)
35. Yoo, P.D., Kim, M.H., Jan, T.: Machine learning techniques and use of event information for stock market prediction: a survey and evaluation. In: International Conference on Computational Intelligence for Modelling, Control and Automation and International Conference on Intelligent Agents, Web Technologies and Internet Commerce (CIMCA-IAWTIC 2006), vol. 2, pp. 835–841. IEEE (2005)
36. Yu, X., Han, B., Yao, J., Niu, G., Tsang, I., Sugiyama, M.: How does disagreement help generalization against label corruption? In: International Conference on Machine Learning, pp. 7164–7173. PMLR (2019)
37. Zhang, X., Li, A., Pan, R.: Stock trend prediction based on a new status box method and AdaBoost probabilistic support vector machine. Appl. Soft Comput. **49**, 385–398 (2016)

SATMeas - Object Detection and Measurement: Canny Edge Detection Algorithm

Satyam Mishra(✉) ⓘ and Le Trung Thanh

International School, Vietnam National University, Hanoi, Vietnam
satyam.entrprnr@gmail.com, thanh.le@vnu.edu.vn

Abstract. In today's modern world, detecting objects in real-time and measuring their dimensions has become a challenge in many areas of industry. Many big warehouses, courier companies, airport containers at airports etc. cannot always get precise/accurate measurement using human hands. In our research we have developed an application SATMeas to detect the object and give the measurements of the object in real-time. We have utilized the canny edge detection algorithm; we made some morphological changes to improve the algorithm to obtain the desired changes. These morphological procedures we did are combination of nonlinear procedures performed generally on the arrangement of pixels without changing their numeral values, erosion and dilation are the keys for morphological operations. We use the OpenCV function cv2.findContours to detect contours by identifying the shapes of the objects inside the edge outline. This is done after edge detection and closing any gaps between edges. We determine pixels per metric variable by relying on a reference object. The Euclidean distance between sets of center points was then determined to get the calculations. Putting it all together, we developed an application SATMeas to detect object in real time and measure it as well. In this way, the outlines of the distinctive objects within the frame were kept. The proposed method works exceptionally quick and efficiently, it gives 98–99% success in determining the measurement of the objects. Hope other scientists can add more features to it and industrialists can commercialize it for better and modern industrial use.

Keywords: OpenCV · Canny edge detection algorithm · Object measurement

1 Introduction

As they explore the world around them, scientists use a variety of abilities. They acquire data using their senses in order to develop observations. Some observations are straightforward. For instance, determining an object's color or texture would be a straightforward observation. However, measurements may be necessary if researchers wish to learn more about a chemical. One of the most basic ideas in science is probably measurement. It would be difficult for scientists to perform experiments or develop ideas without the capacity to measure. In addition to research and the chemical industry, measurement is crucial in a wide range of other professions and activities, including farming, engineering, building, manufacturing, and business. The Greek word "metron," which meaning "restricted proportion," is where the term "measuring" originates. The process of measurement involves comparing an object's characteristics to a standard to ascertain its attributes. Tools are needed for measurements, which also provide scientists a number. A quantity is a way to express how much or how many of anything there is. Using a ruler to determine an object's length is a nice illustration of measuring. Whatever you are measuring is the object, the quantity you are attempting to quantify is the object's length, and the reference point you are using to compare the object's length to is the ruler [1].

The field of computer vision known as object detection allows a system to search a picture for the presence of an object. Applications for object detection include monitoring, surveillance, and industrial inspection, to mention a few. When an object is detected, its characteristics are extracted from the object's picture. After receiving the query picture, the feature extraction technique is applied to it, and the features of the object to be identified are then searched for in the altered query image. If a good match is discovered, it may be concluded that the object is visible in the search picture.

Edges are characteristics that all things have. Numerous edge detection techniques have been suggested in the literature, including the Canny edge detector [2], Prewitt operators [2], Roberts cross-gradient operators [3], and Sobel operators [2]. The canny edge detector is employed in the implementation of this study since studies on the effectiveness of these edge detectors have been conducted [4, 5].

A few edge detection methods for image segmentation have also been investigated in the past. Using MATLAB, several edge detection approaches were used to a picture in the paper [6]. It was found that the edge maps produced by the Marr-Hildreth, LoG, and Canny edge detectors are almost identical. When compared to all other results for the chosen picture, the Canny result is preferable because different edge detection methods perform better in various environments. Although there are several edge detection approaches documented in the literature, it is difficult for the research community to identify the precise picture without artifacts from the original image. In all of computer vision and image processing, the Canny edge detector is likely the most well-known and often used edge detector [6].

Object detection and measurement are often utilized in the industry's product quality stages, where we must either verify the quality or learn the measurement of a tool or object. The proposed research method can be successfully used in practical applications across several sectors. For useful and time-saving application in industries, the study may be utilized to recognize objects in the actual world and measure their dimensions. Utilizing real picture input from a Redmi Note 7 Pro mobile camera, the competency of the suggested framework has been shown. This method's execution has a high calculation rate and is dependent on the choice of frames. Putting it all together, we developed an application SATMeas to detect object in real time and measure it as well to solve the object measurement problem in the real world, some places like big warehouses where it's so tough to measure the size of boxes using human hand.

2 Methods

2.1 General Idea

It is ideally great to be able to distinguish different objects and set them apart from the foundation. We must first identify the reference object in order to compute the estimate for each object. The estimate of additional objects will then be determined using the measurements of the reference objects. An object in the input picture must first be calibrated using a reference object in order for us to establish its size. The width or height of the reference object, expressed in a measured unit, should be known to us (such as millimeters, inches, etc.). This reference object should be easy to find in the input image, either based on the layout of the object (for example, the reference object always being positioned in the top-left corner of the input image) or by appearances (like being a particular color or shape, one of a kind and diverse from all other objects within the picture). Our reference should be interestingly recognizable in both scenarios in a few different ways. As in our research, we used a two-rupee coin, which is the unit of currency for the Indian nation. In order to make it simple for us to extract the two Indian national rupee coin by sorting contours based on their locations, we utilized it as our reference object and made sure it was always positioned as the left-most object in the picture (see Fig. 1 below). The breadth of a two Indian national rupee is 1.07 inches.

Fig. 1. We used a two Indian national rupee coin as our reference object

By ensuring the coin is the left-most object, we are able to sort our object contours from left-to-right, grab the coin (which is able continuously be the primary contour within the sorted list), and utilize it to characterize our pixels_per_metric, which we characterize as:

$$pixels_{per}metric = object_s width / known_{obj} width$$

For example, our two-rupee coin's known width is 1.07 inches and let us suppose that our object_width in pixels is 150 pixels wide (based on its associated bounding box).

Therefore,

$$pixels_{per} metric = \frac{150\,px}{1.07\,in.} = 140.18\,px$$

Thus, it implies that there are approximately 140.18 pixels per every 1.07 inches in our input image. We can use this ratio to calculate the size of object in our input image.

2.2 Platform and Technology Used

PycharM

- PyCharm [7] is an integrated development environment (IDE) used in computer programming, specifically for the Python programming language.
- It provides code analysis, a graphical debugger, an integrated unit tester, integration with version control systems (VCSes), and supports web development with Django as well as data science with Anaconda.
- PyCharm is cross-platform, with Windows, macOS and Linux versions.

OpenCV

- OpenCV [8] (Open-Source Computer Vision Library) is a library of programming functions mainly aimed at real-time computer vision.
- OpenCV runs on the following desktop operating systems: Windows, Linux, macOS, FreeBSD, NetBSD, OpenBSD.
- OpenCV is written in C++ and its primary interface is in C++, but it still retains a less comprehensive though extensive older C interface. All of the new developments and algorithms appear in the C++ interface. There are bindings in Python, Java and MATLAB/OCTAVE.

Numpy

- NumPy [9] is a library for the Python programming language, adding support for large, multi-dimensional arrays and matrices, along with a large collection of high-level mathematical functions to operate on these arrays.
- NumPy targets the CPython reference implementation of Python, which is a non-optimizing bytecode interpreter. Mathematical algorithms written for this version of Python often run much slower than compiled equivalents due to the absence of compiler optimization.
- NumPy addresses the slowness problem partly by providing multidimensional arrays and functions and operators that operate efficiently on arrays; using these requires rewriting some code, mostly inner loops, using NumPy.

Scipy

- SciPy [10] provides algorithms for optimization, integration, interpolation, eigenvalue problems, algebraic equations, differential equations, statistics and many other classes of problems.

imutils

- A series of convenience functions to make basic image processing functions such as translation, rotation, resizing, skeletonization, displaying Matplotlib images, sorting contours, detecting edges, and much easier with OpenCV and both Python 2.7 and Python 3 [11]

argparse

- The argparse [12] module makes it easy to write user-friendly command-line interfaces.
- The program defines what arguments it requires, and argparse will figure out how to parse those out of sys.argv.
- The argparse module also automatically generates help and usage messages and issues errors when users give the program invalid arguments.

2.3   Object Detection and Object Measurement

The study consists of two parts which are object detection and object measurement. For the first part, we use the camera to get the proper input image. And for the second part, OpenCV features will be applied to the input image to detect the object in input image, later determining the dimension of the object. The object which will be detected will quickly be processed to calculate and display the dimensions of the objects.

In our study, firstly, we get our input image. We convert the image to grayscale to have efficiency and accuracy. Objects will be detected using canny edge detector algorithm. We use canny edge detector algorithm to detect single or multiple objects in an image or video. Utilizing canny edge detector algorithms, converted image will be ready to process further as you can also see in Fig. 2.

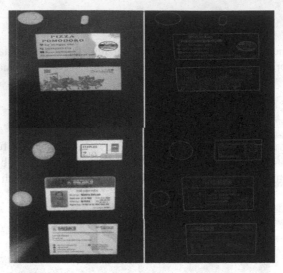

Fig. 2. Example of how original image and canny edge detection applied

After we are done scanning the whole input image using canny edge detector algorithm [13], we execute dilation and erosion algorithm to close holes amount edges in the edge frame, you can see the code snippet in Fig. 3.

```
# perform edge detection, then perform a dilation + erosion to
# close gaps in between object edges
edged = cv2.Canny(gray, 50, 100)
edged = cv2.dilate(edged, None, iterations=1)
edged = cv2.erode(edged, None, iterations=1)
```

Fig. 3. Snippet of code performing edge detection, dilation and erosion

First thing that happens when we apply canny edge detection algorithm is that it starts to delete the noise in the image frames by applying a Gaussian filter. The image after being converted to grayscale and being applied with Gaussian filter can be seen in Fig. 2 example image. Within the compute gradient stage, we identify the edge gradient and direction for each pixel. For the characterizing the gradient at every pixel of smoothed outline, Sobel operator is utilized. A total check of frame will be done a while later receiving gradient size and direction, to dispose of any undesirable pixels which might not set up the edge. Only local maxima must be taken into account as edges at this point by using non-maximum suppression. Non-maximum suppression exchanges the smoothed edges within the frame of the gradient magnitudes to sharpen the edges. Non-maximum suppression is carried out to keep every local maximum within the gradient picture and expelling the whole thing else [14].

The ultimate stage of canny edge detector algorithm is hysteresis thresholding. This stage chooses which edges are without a doubt edge and which aren't edges. The two threshold values are observationally chosen, and their definition will be upon the substance of a given frame. Usually accomplished via choosing enormous and little edge values. On the off chance that Edge pixels stronger than the big threshold, it is marked such as sturdy. Strong edges will be measured as the final edges. Moreover, edge pixel will be smothered In case an edge pixel's weaker than the small threshold, and it is checked as frail edge in case an edge pixel among the enormous and little thresholds [15].

To get the way better result and more precise object detection, the canny edge detection strategy has been improved with a few Morphological operations. These procedures are commonly a combination of nonlinear procedures performed generally on the arrangement of pixels without changing their numeral values, erosion and dilation are the keys for morphological operations [16].

In this research, a morphological process is performed such as a blend of dilation and erosion. The opening is the initial procedure in which erosion is taken after through dilation. Closing is the second operation in which dilation is followed through erosion. As a blend of these processes, we are capable to obtain prevalent assurance for discovery edges in-depth frame.

To briefly summarize object measurement, after edge detection and close any gaps between edges, we detect contours by utilizing an OpenCV function that is cv2.findContours to discover the shapes of the objects within the edge outline. We organize contours from left to right. The reference object within the frame is for all time the left one. We calibrate the camera and choose the parameter value based on the reference object. Following, we check each contour, begin looping over each individual contours. After that, a green rectangle will be drawn around the objects. So, the points of the bounding box rectangle will draw in a little purple round. After that, we will get midpoints since the bounding box is requested. At last, we calculate pixels per metric variable through dependence on reference object. The hD (height) and wD (width) variables will be set according to the height and width distances in pixels, respectively. At that point, we calculated the Euclidean distance among sets of center points.

3   Results

We have successfully developed an application of canny edge detection algorithm for object detection and measurement for multiple purposes including industrial use as well. We proposed the system to measure objects in a real time pictures. We arranged many test setups to test the rightness of the proposed strategy. The implemented proposed framework has made by the assistance of Python programming language. The camera has been successfully taking pictures for the experiments. The proposed system applies four operations such as record frames, find edges, find objects, and measure size for each object. When we run the application, the output screen displays on the PC screen as appear in Fig. 4 below and Fig. 5 shows the object detection and measurements after applying of the algorithm. Each size of an object is calculated and displayed.

Fig. 4. Output display on my screen

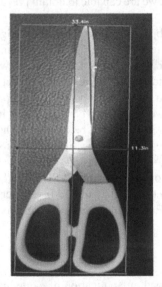

Fig. 5. Display of the object measurement after application of algorithm

In the first test, we calculated the size of objects such as coin, scissor, medicine tablet, college id. Table 1, shows the accuracy of proposed object measurement system for these objects. Abbreviations in the table are as follows; RMH: Real Measured Height, EMH: Expected Measured Height, RMW: Real Measured Width, EMW: Expected Measured Width.

Table 1. Accuracy of object measurement.

Name of objects	RMH (in)	EMH (in)	RMW (in)	EMW (in)	Accuracy
Scissor	11.5	11.3	33.4	33.5	98%
Coin	1.07	1.0	1.07	1.0	93%
Medicine tablet	0.4	0.3	0.8	0.7	99%
College ID card	2.95	2.8	4.75	4.6	99%

The error in measurement is very low. The error rate is specifically much smaller when camera is above the objects or 90°.

3.1 Advantages

1) Reduces human error and provides efficiency.
2) It is easily usable, it's user-friendly.
3) The less the error is you will get more work done in less time.
4) Cheap solution.

3.2 Disadvantages

There is a need for a backup system to store or back up any record.

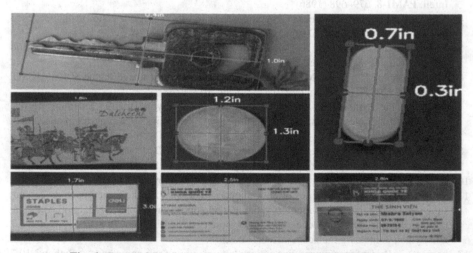

Fig. 6. Some of the objects tested for their measurement in our study

Figure 6 above shows how accurately and precisely our application SATMeas detects and measures the dimensions of the object.

4   Conclusion

In this research, a capable object measurement method is proposed for industrial frame-works. Within the offered system, Computer Vision utilized to distinguish and measure objects. The framework can identify and measure objects. After the object has been iden-tified by utilizing canny edge detector algorithm, the measure is gotten for each object by utilizing OpenCV functions. We upgraded the canny edge detector algorithm through utilizing Morphological operations. This procedure benefits to dispense with additional noises. Moreover, whereas eliminating the additional noises it moreover smoothens the shape and keeps the layout and estimate of each object. Putting it all together, we devel-oped an application SATMeas to detect object in real time and measure it as well. In this way, the outlines of the distinctive objects within the frame were kept. The proposed method works exceptionally quick and efficiently, it gives 98–99% success in determin-ing the measurement of the objects. Hope other scientists can add more features to it and industrialists can commercialize it for better and modern industrial use.

References

1. Importance of measurement in science - Google Search. https://www.google.com/sea rch?rlz=1C1CHBF_enVN959VN959&q=Importance+of+measurement+in+science&sa= X&ved=2ahUKEwirorXZ1Zb6AhU3mVYBHdqeDV0Q1QJ6BAgrEAE&biw=1280&bih= 781&dpr=0.8. Accessed 15 Sept 2022
2. Gonzalez, R.C.: Digital Image Processing. Pearson Education India (2009)
3. Canny, J.: A computational approach to edge detection. IEEE Trans. Pattern Anal. Mach. Intell. **PAMI-8**, 679–698 (1986)
4. Shrivakshan, G.T., Chandrasekar, C.: A comparison of various edge detection techniques used in image processing. Int. J. Comput. Sci. Issues (IJCSI) **9**, 269 (2012)
5. Nadernejad, E., Sharifzadeh, S., Hassanpour, H.: Edge detection techniques: evaluations and comparisons. Appl. Math. Sci. **2**, 1507–1520 (2008)
6. Muthukrishnan, R., Radha, M.: Edge detection techniques for image segmentation. IJCSIT **3**, 259–267 (2011). https://doi.org/10.5121/ijcsit.2011.3620
7. PyCharm: the Python IDE for Professional Developers by JetBrains | JetBrains: Devel-oper Tools for Professionals and Teams. https://www.jetbrains.com/lp/pycharm-anaconda/. Accessed 15 Sept 2022
8. Home – OpenCV. https://opencv.org/. Accessed 15 Sept 2022
9. numpy · PyPI. https://pypi.org/project/numpy/. Accessed 15 Sept 2022
10. scipy: SciPy: Scientific Library for Python. https://www.scipy.org
11. Rosebrock, A.: imutils: a series of convenience functions to make basic image processing functions such as translation, rotation, resizing, skeletonization, displaying Matplotlib images, sorting contours, detecting edges, and much more easier with OpenCV and both Python 2.7 and Python 3. https://github.com/jrosebr1/imutils
12. argparse — Parser for command-line options, arguments and sub-commands — Python 3.10.7 documentation. https://docs.python.org/3/library/argparse.html. Accessed 15 Sept 2022
13. OpenCV: Canny Edge Detection. https://docs.opencv.org/4.x/da/d22/tutorial_py_canny.html. Accessed 15 Sept 2022

14. Canny Edge Detection Step by Step in Python — Computer Vision | by Sofiane Sahir | Towards Data Science. https://towardsdatascience.com/canny-edge-detection-step-by-step-in-python-computer-vision-b49c3a2d8123. Accessed 15 Sept 2022
15. Kumar, M., Saxena, R.: Algorithm and technique on various edge detection: a survey. Signal Image Process. **4**, 65 (2013)
16. Image Processing in Python - Edge Detection, Resizing, Erosion, and Dilation – AskPython. https://www.askpython.com/python/examples/image-processing-in-python. Accessed 15 Sept 2022

Multi-Classification of Electric Power Metadata based on Prompt-tuning

Xiao Liang[1], Wensi Zhang[1], Shuya Lei[1], Yifang Zhang[2(✉)], Moxuan Xu[2], Liangying Peng[3], and Jun Feng[3]

[1] State Grid Smart Grid Research Institute Co., Ltd., Beijing, China
[2] School of Cyber Science and Engineering, University of International Relations, Beijing, China
zhang1fang@foxmail.com
[3] State Grid Zhejiang Information and Telecommunication Branch, Zhejiang, China

Abstract. In the era of big data, massive amounts of data are generated every day, especially in industrial fields, such as electricity, communications, finance, meteorology, satellites, etc. These industrial data are rich in value, and will be the foundation of digital economy and information management. Due to the particularity of the industry, the exploitation of big data mainly faces the following challenges that degrade the performance of mainstream general models: 1. The text classification model needs to be universal and rapidly deployed; 2. The short text in the metadata contains large amounts of jargons that are difficult to be semantically vectorized. To this end, this paper proposes a pre-training model based on prompt-tuning, targeting on the classification of metadata for the power industry. The model consists of three modules: 1. Continual pre-training module conducts the mask and prediction task on the unlabeled text dataset of the power industry to enable the pre-training model to acquire new vocabulary and knowledge of the industry; 2. The prompt-tuning model uses the continuous depth prompt technology as the backbone, which helps to bring the pre-training model closer to the downstream tasks. 3. The exterior knowledge-based verbalizer model extends the tags to make the text generation model perform better. The model was tested on a real dataset from the power industry, and was able to improve the F1-score by 13.86% and 6.02%, compared to the classification model based on deep learning and the p-tuning model without knowledgeable verbalizer, respectively.

Keywords: Pre-train · Prompt · Short-text classification · Multi-classification

1 Introduction

With the development and popularization of smart grid, power system has entered the era of big data [1–3]. Metadata is data that describes data which mainly describe data properties, and thus be used to support database functions such as indicating storage location, indexing historical data, searching resources, and recording file [4]. Metadata management is the foundation of big data governance [5]. To effectively analyze and

X. Pan et al. (Eds.): AIMS 2022, LNCS 13729, pp. 102–114, 2022.
https://doi.org/10.1007/978-3-031-23504-7_8

manage the above industrial metadata has become the basis of digital economy development [6]. Therefore, we need a classification model with high performance and high availability to effectively improve the data management capability of manufacturing enterprises.

The current text classification model is difficult to solve the following problems due to the industry particularity: 1. There is extreme difficulty in the expansion of industrial datasets because its annotation heavily relies on expert knowledge, which will seriously degrade the performance when fine-tuning with mainstream classification models; 2. The metadata in industrial big data is mostly composed of short text that contains a large number of industry jargons and domain knowledge, which is difficult to be semantically represented [7].

Table 1. Six categories of electric power metadata.

Metadata category	Subclass
Regex	Postcode, Phone call, ID, Date
Text	Address, Name, Company Name
Enumeration	Numeric enumeration, Chinese enumeration
Numbers	Percentage, Amount of money,
Code	Generative code, Long code, Other code
Notes	Any short text

In this paper, the proposed model is built upon a read industrial metadata dataset collected from power industry, including around 4,000 samples. The metadata of power system is divided into six categories, as shown in Table 1.

Therefore, this paper proposed to apply pre-training and prompt-tuning for multi-classification on short text industrial dataset (e.g., power industry). Compared with traditional classification baselines without pre-training and prompting paradigm, or p-tuning ablation models without introduction of external knowledge, our model improves 13.86% and 6.02% absolute scores on macro-F1, respectively.

The main contribution of this paper can be summarized as follows:

(1) We apply continuous depth prompt to short text classification tasks, and the effect is better than fine-tuning.
(2) To enhance the verbalizer module, we redesign Label Sets by sub-tags contained in metadata.
(3) The experiment proves the effectiveness of our model in low-cost metadata management.

2 Related Works

This paper mainly studies the text multi-classification task over power system metadata. The work is related to at least three lines of research: metadata, short text classification and prompt.

2.1 Short Text Classification

Text classification is one of the most fundamental and important tasks in the field of natural language processing [8]. Due to the success of deep learning, related research in this area has proliferated in past last decade, and datasets and evaluation metrics are approaching maturity [9].

Multi-grained attention network for aspect-level sentiment classification employs a multi-grained attention network that combines coarse-grained and fine-grained attention to capture the interaction between aspect and context at the word level [10]; aspect alignment loss is used to describe the aspect-level interaction between aspects that share a common context [11]. Joint embedding of words and labels for text classification further introduces an attentional framework that measures the compatibility of embeddings between text sequences and labels [12], and treats text classification as a label-word joint embedding problem: each label is embedded in the same vector space together with a word vector. Deep contextualized word representations introduce a novel form of deep contextual word representation that models both (1) complex features of word usage (e.g., syntax and semantics); (2) the way these usages change between linguistic contexts (i.e., modeling polysemy) [13]. Its word vector is a learning function of the internal state of a deep bidirectional language model, which has been pre-trained on a large text corpus [14]. BERT [15] is able to learn sentence relational representations with negative sampling at sentence level. Thus, only one additional output layer is needed to fine-tune the pre-trained BERT representation in order to create state-of-the-art models for various tasks [16]. However, with the increasing number of parameters of the pre-training model, it is more desirable for the model to achieve excellent performance with few-shot or even zero-shot [17]. However, due to the lack of training data in the pre-training model, it is difficult to obtain excellent performance through finetuning. In this case, prompt has been proposed and received wide attention.

2.2 Prompt

During 2017–2019, the focus of natural language processing researchers has gradually shifted from the traditional task-specific supervised model to pre-training. The idea of pre-training-based language models is usually "pre-train, fine-tune", which means when applying PLMs to downstream tasks, designing training objects and tuning PLM ontologies according to downstream tasks in the pre-training and fine-tuning phases.

With the growth of PLM, the hardware requirements, data requirements and actual costs of fine tune are also rising [18]. In addition, the rich and diverse downstream tasks also make the design of pre-training and fine-tuning stage complicated. Therefore, researchers hope to explore a smaller, lighter, more universal and efficient method. Prompt is an attempt in this direction.

The new model integrated with prompt can be roughly summarized as "pre-train, prompt, and predict "[19]. In this mode, the downstream task is readjusted to the form similar to the pretraining task. Its research has two different paradigms: the fine tuning based on prompt is inspired by PET papers, and the key point is to further optimize the parameters [20]. This method is considered to be a way to better few-shot learners of small language models; different prompt (discrete/continuous) is directly used to adjust parameters and use them in different downstream tasks [21].

Since then, researchers have noticed the relevant content of manual design of answer in prompt learning [22]. Like manual construction of prompt, the way of manual design of answer is likely to ultimately obtain a suboptimal language model, which still depends on the knowledge of professionals and is not easy to migrate to more scenes. Therefore, the work of automatic answer search came into being.

2.3 Verbalizer

Answer paraphrasing is a kind of method that first initializes an answer space and then expands the space with the interpretation of these answers until it converges [23]. Considering that a single answer candidate may not be stable, if the language model does not understand it well, it will lead to a large deviation in the final result. The answer space is expanded by back translation to obtain multiple candidate expressions of each category [24]. A more robust result can be obtained by comprehensively considering the prediction results of the model for multiple candidate expressions. Prune-then-search method is to first generate the initial pruning answer space of several trusted answers [25], and then further search on this pruning space through the algorithm to select the final group of answers. When extracting relations, Label Decomposition automatically decomposes each relation label into its constituent words and takes them as the answer. The probability of the answer span will be calculated as the sum of the probabilities of each token [26].

It is very challenging for PET to manually define the mapping from categories to single tokens, because it requires not only that category knowledge be expressed as single tokens in natural language, but also that MLM language model effectively understand the tokens. For this reason, it is very important to select appropriate single tokens for each category.

Few works discuss the use of soft answer tokens, which can also be optimized through gradient descent. Hambardzumayan et al. assigned a virtual token to each class tag, and optimized the virtual token embedding and prompt token embedding of each class [27]. Because response tokens are directly optimized in the embedding space, they do not use LM learning embedding, but learn the embedding of each tag from scratch.

3 Methodology

In this section, we first formulate the short text multi-classification task, and then introduce our methodology with corresponding modules.

3.1 Task Formulation

In this paper, we denote the database for the short text classification task in the electric power industry as D. The short texts can be denoted as $\{X_1, X_2, \cdots, X_n\}$, and the labels can represent as $\{L_1, L_2, \cdots, L_6\}$, respectively corresponding to type

{*Regex, Text, Enumeration, Numbers, Code, Notes*}. Each short text has only one specific label corresponding to it, so each data can be expressed as $\{X_i, L_{i,j}\}, i \in (1, 2, \cdots, n), j \in (1, 2, \cdots, 6)$. Each short text has been tokenized into Chinese words, which can be written as $X_i = (w_1, w_2, \cdots, w_n)$. Given short text X_i, a short text classification model is required to predict a label $\{L_{i,j}\}$. Based on formulated defination, we propose the DPT-BERT model, which is composed of three parts: continual pre-training module, deep prompt-tuning module and exterior knowledge-based verbalizer module.

3.2 Pre-trained Model with Electric Power Knowledge

Pre-training paradigms are widely used in NLP. General large-scale encoders (e.g., Bert, Roberta, and T5) are mainly pre-trained on universal corpus such as Wikipedia or social media text, and thus perform well on tasks concerning general text. However, in this paper, the short text metadata from the power industry consists of large amount jargons that rarely exposed in general corpus [28]. To fix the domain exposure gap, we proposed to incorporate large scale unlabeled power data for continual pre-training.

We choose RoBERTa-wwm-ext-large-Chinese[1] as the starting checkpoint. According to Cui et al. [29], this checkpoint is a RoBERTa-like BERT instead of original RoBERTa model. Therefore, our subsequent use still follows the BERT processing strategies. The Next Sentence Prediction task is abandoned as many works have proved its unnecessity. In the pre-training stage, the model is trained with Whole Word Mask (wwm), which is particularly mask all the Chinese characters that make up the same word. The use of wwm is not only suitable for the actual semantic information of Chinese word segmentation, but also similar to our downstream task, the prediction task based on prompt templates.

Figure 1 demonstrates our continual pre-training module. We input the text to the pre-training model for masked token prediction. At the same time, the vocabulary of the pre-training model is updated according to newly input text.

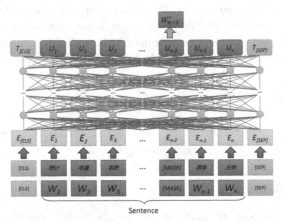

Fig. 1. Continue pre-training on RoBERTa-wwm-ext-large.

---

[1] https://github.com/ymcui/Chinese-BERT-wwm.

3.3 Deep Prompt-Tuning Module

The original prompt templates are generally discrete and interpretable prompt statements, but the effects of different templates vary greatly [30]. It is very difficult to find the template with the best performance under existing conditions [31]. On the other hand, discrete tokens are difficult to fine-tune the paradigm, and natural language templates are searched in discrete space, which means the effect is limited. The core idea of prompt-tuning is to build an appropriate prefix/suffix to keep downstream tasks consistent with the pre-training tasks, so as to achieve good performances in zero-shot and few-shot tasks. It has been proven that continuous vector-based templates can have similar effects compared with discrete language-based templates.

We developed our prompt-tuning strategy with vector-based prompt [32]. As shown in Fig. 2, we add 25 prepositional vectors on the 17–24th layers of RoBERTa-wwm-ext-large model. Because of the bidi-head attention mechanism of BERT, we no longer need to determine the mask position, but just use the LM head for the prediction of the label of multi-classification task. It is the same as the general finetuning task in classifying tasks. After each parameter is initialized randomly, MLP reparameterization is used to optimize its performance.

Continuous prompt generally inserts continuous vectors into the input embedding sequence of the first layer of the transformer, and the vectors on the subsequent prompt positions are calculated from the previous layer to finally obtain the prediction results of the mask positions. This will lead to limited parameters that we can adjust, and there are many nonlinear activation functions in the middle layer of the multi-layer deep network, which will make it difficult to predict the adjustment results of the first layer of the prompt, and thus increase the difficulty of optimizing parameters [33].

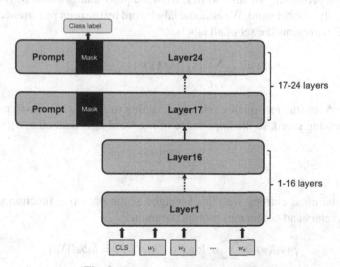

Fig. 2. Deep prompt tuning on LM.

3.4 Exterior Knowledge-Based Verbalizer

In prompt learning, label word mapping (verbalizer) is critical to convert the prediction of in-vocabulary words at [MASK] position into classification tags. If we do not expand the label, the single label text may degrade the classification performance due to its shallow and limited text meaning [34]. Since general knowledge base is not tailored for domain-specific pre-training models, synonym lexicon, back translation or other knowledge base methods will introduce heavy noise during the expansion. For example, the remark extended by TEXT may be highly correlated with NOTE, thus causing confusion; Or Regex, as a professional vocabulary, is difficult to find meaningful synonyms in semantics, and thus simple expansion will make corrupt the core meaning of the label.

Shown as Table 1, subcategory terms are labelled alongside with corresponding major categories (e.g., Postcode, Phone call, ID, Date and other subcategories in the Regex class), we supposed to conduct label expansion with subcategory metadata. Compared with synonyms, the subcategory information can obtain knowledge beyond the semantics. If there is no sub tag like Phone call and ID, some Regex text will be easy to be classified into another number class, while the classification will be more accurate by introducing sub tags. However, the introduction of subcategories is not customized for the pre-training language model. During labeling, we need to delete words that are of low quality for the model. Since the total amount data of different subcategories in the same major category is quite different, we attach weights to them during training to enhance classification performance.

The output probability of label word L from the pre-training model M is used as the prior probability of label word. We estimate label word by the prior occurrence frequency as follows. C represents the set of all labels.

The output probability of label word L from the pre-training model M is used as the prior probability of label word. We estimate label word by the prior occurrence frequency as follows. C represents the set of all labels.

$$P(L) \approx \frac{1}{C} \sum_{x \in C} P_M \left([MASK] = label | X_p \right) \tag{1}$$

After we delete the low-quality sub tag according to $P(L)$, we can assign a learnable weight to each tag saved, so the importance of tag word L_i is defined as α_i:

$$\alpha_i = \frac{exp(w_i)}{\sum_{j \in L} exp(w_j)} \tag{2}$$

We use the cross entropy with label weight as the objective function to optimize weight parameters and continuous prompt parameters.

$$p(y|X_P) = \sum \alpha_i \log P_M \left([MASK] = label | X_p \right) \tag{3}$$

The weighted average of the tag word scores is used as the prediction score to determine the text classification.

4   Experiment

To verify the effectiveness of our proposed method, we conduct a series of experiments on a real dataset of the power industry. In this section, we will introduce the experimental dataset, parameters settings, and experimental metrics. We also make an analysis for the experimental results.

4.1   Dataset

The experimental dataset is based on the National Grid electricity business data, which is aggregated from different levels of data management systems. The dataset contains a total of 4,108 data and corresponding tags are manually labeled by experts. These six subsets $\{L_1, L_2, L_3, L_4, L_5, L_6\}$ are respectively comprised of 1446, 810, 484, 504, 217, 647 items of short text. Compared with conventional data sets, the volume of this dataset is seriously insufficient and there is a problem of data imbalance.

4.2   Parameter Settings

We conducted our experiments with system of Ubuntu 16.04, CPU of Intel Xeon 218, GPU of Nvidia V100S. The development environment we used is Pytorch 1.12, development tool is vim, development language is Python. Parameters of pre-training model RoBERTa-wwm-ext-large, Chinese are shown in Table 2.

Table 2.   Basic parameters of the model.

Parameters	Value	Parameters	Value
Max-length	256	Learning-rate	3e−5
Optimizer	AdamW	Epochs	3
Training times	2000	Batch size	128

4.3   Evaluation Metrics

F1-score is a statistical indicator used to measure the accuracy of binary classification model. However, new indicators need to be introduced to measure the overall classification performance of the model. Due to the data imbalance in our dataset, we choose macro-F1 to compare the performance gap between different models. The weight of each category is same in macro-F1 calculation, which will not be affected by data imbalance. It can avoid the indicators only reflect the classification effect of the category with larger data scale.

In multi-classification tasks, precision and recall of each six categories can be calculated separately. We get F1-Score$_i$ of six categories according to the following formula:

$$F1 - \text{Score}_i = \frac{2 \cdot \text{Precision}_i \cdot \text{Recall}_i}{\text{Precision}_i + \text{Recall}_i} i \in (1, 2, \cdots, 6) \tag{4}$$

We get Precision$_m$ and Recall$_m$ of the whole model by the following formula:

$$\text{Precision}_m = \frac{\sum_{i=1}^{6} \text{Precision}_i}{6} \tag{5}$$

$$\text{Recall}_m = \frac{\sum_{i=1}^{6} \text{Recall}_i}{6} \tag{6}$$

Then we can get *macro-F*1 of the model according to the following formula:

$$macro - F1 = \frac{\sum_{i=1}^{6} \text{F1} - \text{Score}_i}{6} \tag{7}$$

4.4 Experiments

We use ten-fold data by dividing the dataset into ten equal-sized parts, each with approximately 410. One out of ten parts is used as the test set, and the remaining nine parts are used as a training set, then we get the average of ten training results. This method can circumvent randomness during training, while fully validating the stability of the model. To evaluate the performance of every specific module, we further conduct a series of ablation experiments.

Continual Pre-training Model. As shown in Table 3, FastText represents short texts as word vectors and uses SVM models for classification; the RoBERTa relies on Chinese Wikipedia, and other encyclopedias, news, Q&A for pre-training; eRoBERTa refers to continual pre-training rely on no-label text of power industry based on RoBERTa; Both of RoBert and eRoBERTa fine-tuning on the classification task after adding the linear head. DPT-RoBERTa uses eRoBERTa with freeze parameters and prompt-tuning (Table 4).

Table 3. The results of power metadata multi-classification experiment.

Model	FastText	RoBERTa	eRoBERTa	DPT-RoBERTa
Precision	0.6838	0.7304	0.7714	0.8606
Recall	0.6916	0.7250	0.7929	0.8700
F1-Score	0.6760	0.7239	0.7761	0.8625

FastText cannot learn semantic knowledge, which leads to poor effect. eRoBERTa that has been continuously pre-trained on the texts of power industry has significantly better performance (5.22% on macro F1) than the original RoBERTa, which confirms the truth that large-scale self-supervised continual pre-training on the domain-replated corpus has advantage in the downstream classification task of the power industry. Compared with eRoBERTa of fine-tuning, prompt-based DPT-Roberta further improves the results by 8.64% in macro-F1 respectively, and has advantages in small sample training. When the amount of overall fine-tuned parameters is less than 1% of the original model, the convergence speed is faster and the effect is better.

Table 4. The results of inserting prompt at different layers.

Layers	1−24	1−8	1−16	17−24	9−24
Precision	0.8128	0.7544	0.7912	0.8117	0.7894
Recall	0.8025	0.7539	0.8174	0.8067	0.8061
F1-Score	0.8062	0.7493	0.7894	0.8023	0.7900

Deep Prompt-Tuning Module. We conducted experiments on the hyperparameters of continuous prompt, and adjusted the number of layers of deep prompt and the number of prompt vectors respectively.

We find that the performance of the model depth is basically the best under the condition of 17–24 layers, and there is a little difference from the full layer adjustment of 1–24 layers. If only the initial layers, such as 1–8 and 1–16, are fine-tuned, their performance is significantly weaker than fine-tuning the post layers. We believe the shallow layers of BERT are more responsible for the understanding of more basic unit words such as word embedding, while the deeper layers are responsible for the contextual connection and the understanding of deep semantics such as dependency relations. Therefore, it is basically the best that we establish continuous adjustable prompt templates in the last eight layers to be responsible for the constraint effect of the mask position (Table 5).

Table 5. The results of inserting prompt with different length.

Tokens	10	15	20	25	30
Precision	0.7751	0.7620	0.7775	0.8117	0.7937
Recall	0.7703	0.7590	0.7643	0.8067	0.8167
F1-Score	0.7710	0.75573	0.7649	0.8023	0.7996

We also study the length of the template. It is shown in Table 5 that the impact of length on the performance of model is not stable. If the length is too short, the constraint of the template on model will be insufficient. If the length is too long, the template cannot be effectively adjusted because of our small amount of data. If the initialization is improper, the best parameters will not be found.

Exterior Knowledge-Based Verbalizer. Model performance of text classification and other tasks is greatly affected by the expansion of label. We tested the forward mentioned eRoBERTa base on prompt as follows. Raw Tag refers to use the original six types of tags; Subclasses means that we simply introduce all the sub tags into the model without adjustment, and directly determine the classification attribution from the sub tags; Chosen sub refers to the classification task after filtering and removing the interfering sub tags; Chosen w-sub means that we add adjustable weights to each sub tag during few-shot training.

Table 6. Label engineering on deep prompt tuning.

Labels	Raw Tag	Subclasses	Chosen sub	Chosen w-sub
Precision	0.8117	0.7620	0.8347	0.8606
Recall	0.8067	0.7590	0.8320	0.8700
F1-Score	0.8023	0.7557	0.8313	0.8625

The performance of the model with label without adjustment will decline by 4.66% in F1-score since different sub labels may cause conflicts in the general category of the major label. Unreasonable sub label construction may cause noise interference to the model (e.g., Subclasses). The sub tags filtered by our model can overtake this problem. For simple synonym extension (e.g., Chosen Sub), selecting appropriate sub tags can make tags of the same category have more reasonable semantic scope, which helps the model understanding labels more accurately. After further adding weights to sub tags (e.g., Chosen w-sub), the issue of semantic conflicts between different sub tags in the same class will be solved, and rare tags will be given greater weights.

5 Conclusion

We propose the DPT-RoBERTa model three modules: 1. Continual pre-training module conducts the mask and prediction task on the unlabeled text dataset of the power industry to enable the pre-training model to acquire new vocabulary and knowledge of the industry; 2. The prompt-tuning model uses the continuous depth prompt technology as the backbone, which helps to have more adjustable parameters for better performance when building templates. 3. The exterior knowledge-based verbalizer model extends the tags to bring the pre-training model closer to the downstream tasks.

The model, which is experimented on a real dataset in the electric power industry, can improve macro-F1 by 18.65% compared with the traditional classification model FastText and by 13.86% compared with the BERT pre-training model. The model is able to improve the F1-score by 6.02% compared to the classification model based on deep learning without knowledgeable verbalizer which fully confirms the effectiveness of each module. The experiment proves the effectiveness of our model in low-cost metadata management, which means the DPT-RoBERTa model has a wide application space.

Acknowledgement. This paper is supported by the science and technology project of State Grid Corporation of China: "Study on Intelligent Analysis Technology of Abnormal Power Data Quality based on Rule Mining" (Grand No. 5700-202119176A-0-0-00).

References

1. Fang, X., Misra, S., Xue, G., et al.: Smart grid—the new and improved power grid: a survey. IEEE Commun. Surv. Tutorials **14**(4), 944–980 (2011)
2. Tuballa, M.L., Abundo, M.L.: A review of the development of Smart Grid technologies. Renew. Sustain. Energy Rev. **59**, 710–725 (2016)
3. Daki, H., El Hannani, A., Aqqal, A., et al.: Big data management in smart grid: concepts, requirements and implementation. J. Big Data **4**(1), 1–19 (2017)
4. Introduction to metadata. Getty Publications (2016)
5. Weil, S.A., Pollack, K.T., Brandt, S.A., et al.: Dynamic metadata management for petabyte-scale file systems. In: SC 2004: Proceedings of the 2004 ACM/IEEE conference on Supercomputing, p. 4. IEEE (2004)
6. Didenko, N.I., Skripnuk, D.F., Mirolyubova, O.V.: Big data and the global economy. In: 2017 Tenth International Conference Management of Large-Scale System Development (MLSD), pp. 1–5. IEEE (2017)
7. Galati, F., Bigliardi, B.: Industry 4.0: emerging themes and future research avenues using a text mining approach. Comput. Ind. **109**, 100–113 (2019)
8. Kowsari, K., Jafari Meimandi, K., Heidarysafa, M., et al.: Text classification algorithms: a survey. Information **10**(4), 150 (2019)
9. Lai, S., Xu, L., Liu, K., et al.: Recurrent convolutional neural networks for text classification. In: Twenty-ninth AAAI Conference on Artificial Intelligence (2015)
10. Wang, S., Huang, M., Deng, Z.: Densely connected CNN with multi-scale feature attention for text classification. In: IJCAI. 2018, pp. 4468–4474 (2018)
11. Fan, F., Feng, Y., Zhao, D.: Multi-grained attention network for aspect-level sentiment classification. In: Proceedings of the 2018 Conference on Empirical Methods in Natural Language Processing, pp. 3433–3442 (2018)
12. Linmei, H., Yang, T., Shi, C., et al.: Heterogeneous graph attention networks for semi-supervised short text classification. In: Proceedings of the 2019 Conference on Empirical Methods in Natural Language Processing and the 9th International Joint Conference on Natural Language Processing (EMNLP-IJCNLP), pp. 4821–4830 (2019)
13. Tenney, I., Xia, P., Chen, B., et al.: What do you learn from context? probing for sentence structure in contextualized word representations. arXiv preprint arXiv:1905.06316 (2019)
14. Peters, M.E., Ammar, W., Bhagavatula, C., et al.: Semi-supervised sequence tagging with bidirectional language models. arXiv preprint arXiv:1705.00108 (2017)
15. Tenney, I., Das, D., Pavlick, E.: BERT rediscovers the classical NLP pipeline. arXiv preprint arXiv:1905.05950 (2019)
16. Sun, C., Qiu, X., Xu, Y., Huang, X.: How to fine-tune bert for text classification? In: Sun, M., Huang, X., Ji, H., Liu, Z., Liu, Y. (eds.) CCL 2019. LNCS (LNAI), vol. 11856, pp. 194–206. Springer, Cham (2019). https://doi.org/10.1007/978-3-030-32381-3_16
17. Hendrycks, D., Lee, K., Mazeika, M.: Using pre-training can improve model robustness and uncertainty. In: International Conference on Machine Learning. PMLR, pp. 2712–2721 (2019)
18. Qin, G., Eisner, J.: Learning how to ask: Querying lms with mixtures of soft prompts. arXiv preprint arXiv:2104.06599 (2021)
19. Liu, P., Yuan, W., Fu, J., et al.: Pre-train, prompt, and predict: a systematic survey of prompting methods in natural language processing. arXiv preprint arXiv:2107.13586 (2021)
20. Gao, T., Fisch, A., Chen, D.: Making pre-trained language models better few-shot learners. arXiv preprint arXiv:2012.15723 (2020)
21. Zhou, K., Yang, J., Loy, C.C., et al.: Learning to prompt for vision-language models. Int. J. Comput. Vision **130**(9), 2337–2348 (2022)

22. Scao, T.L., Rush, A.M.: How many data points is a prompt worth?. arXiv preprint arXiv: 2103.08493 (2021)
23. Jiang, Z., Xu, F.F., Araki, J., et al.: How can we know what language models know? Trans. Assoc. Comput. Linguist. **8**, 423–438 (2020)
24. Ding, N., Hu, S., Zhao, W., et al.: Openprompt: An open-source framework for prompt-learning. arXiv preprint arXiv:2111.01998 (2021)
25. Min, B., Ross, H., Sulem, E., et al.: Recent advances in natural language processing via large pre-trained language models: a survey. arXiv preprint arXiv:2111.01243 (2021)
26. Hu, S., Ding, N., Wang, H., et al.: Knowledgeable prompt-tuning: Incorporating knowledge into prompt verbalizer for text classification. arXiv preprint arXiv:2108.02035 (2021)
27. Hambardzumyan, K., Khachatrian, H., May, J.: Warp: Word-level adversarial reprogramming. arXiv preprint arXiv:2101.00121 (2021)
28. Gururangan, S., Marasović, A., Swayamdipta, S., et al.: Don't stop pretraining: adapt language models to domains and tasks. arXiv preprint arXiv:2004.10964 (2020)
29. Cui, Y., Che, W., Liu, T., et al.: Pre-training with whole word masking for Chinese bert. IEEE/ACM Trans. Audio, Speech Lang. Process. **29**, 3504–3514 (2021)
30. Li, X.L., Liang, P.: Prefix-tuning: Optimizing continuous prompts for generation. arXiv preprint arXiv:2101.00190 (2021)
31. Liu, X., Zheng, Y., Du, Z., et al.: GPT understands, too. arXiv preprint arXiv:2103.10385 (2021)
32. Liu, X., Ji, K., Fu, Y., et al.: P-tuning v2: Prompt tuning can be comparable to fine-tuning universally across scales and tasks. arXiv preprint arXiv:2110.07602 (2021)
33. Jawahar, G., Sagot, B., Seddah, D.: What does BERT learn about the structure of language?. In: ACL 2019–57th Annual Meeting of the Association for Computational Linguistics (2019)
34. Schick, T., Schütze, H.: It's not just size that matters: Small language models are also few-shot learners. arXiv preprint arXiv:2009.07118 (2020)

Dual-Branch Network Fused with Attention Mechanism for Clothes-Changing Person Re-identification

Yong Lu$^{(\boxtimes)}$ and Mingzhe Jin

Minzu University of China, Beijing 100190, China
2006153@muc.edu.cn

Abstract. Clothes-changing person re-identification is a hot issue in the current academic circle. The key to this work is to extract the inherent characteristics of people, such as gait and body shape. Most of the current methods assume that persons' clothes will not change in a short period of time, so these methods are not applicable when changing clothes. Based on this situation, this paper proposes a dual-branch network clothes-changing person re-identification method fused with attention mechanism. The attention mechanism captures and aggregates persons semantic-related information in channels and spaces, and trains the clothes classification branch to suppress Sensitivity of the network to clothing features. In addition, the method in this paper does not use auxiliary means such as human skeleton, and the complexity of the model is greatly reduced. This paper conducts experiments on the popular clothes-changing person re-identification dataset PRCC, and the experimental results show that the method in this paper is more advanced than popular methods. This paper also conducts experiments on LaST, an ultra-large-scale cross-space-time dataset, and also achieves competitive result results.

Keywords: Clothes-changing person re-identification · Attention mechanism · Dual-branch network

1 Introduction

Person re-identification technology is one of the key technologies of intelligent monitoring systems. It can be regarded as an image retrieval problem. It can be used to monitor and search for persons (criminal suspects, lost persons, persons involved in epidemics, etc.), and is an important factor in preventing and combating violent terrorist crimes. It is of great significance to improve the social governance system. Due to the limitations of technology and other factors, most of the current research on person re-identification assumes that the clothes remain unchanged, and extracts features such as color and texture. The target of person re-identification is to search for the target person from surveillance videos of different locations and times. Most existing models [5, 16, 20] assume that persons do not change clothes in a short period of time. However, if you want to re-identify a person for a long time, the problem of changing clothes is unavoidable.

X. Pan et al. (Eds.): AIMS 2022, LNCS 13729, pp. 115–125, 2022.
https://doi.org/10.1007/978-3-031-23504-7_9

In addition, there are also problems of changing clothes in some short-term real-world scenarios, for example, criminal suspects usually change clothes to avoid being identified and tracked. In the clothes-changing scene, the original method will no longer be applicable, because different people may be incorrectly matched if they wear similar clothes. To address this problem, this paper studies the clothes-changing person re-identification.

In order to avoid the interference of clothes, some clothes-changing re-id methods [8, 14, 15, 24, 25] start to append the input of other modalities besides the input image, such as 3D shape [8], bones [24], contours [25] et al. However, these parties often require additional models to capture multimodal information, which undoubtedly increases the complexity of the model. In fact, the original images contain a wealth of clothing-independent information, which is largely underutilized.

In order to better mine the clothes-independent information in the image, this paper adds a channel attention mechanism and a spatial attention mechanism to the model to capture the semantically related information of persons in the channel and space more effectively. At the same time, the influence of irrelevant background is eliminated. And for the influence of clothing features, this paper sets up a clothes classification branch, and suppresses the model's sensitivity to clothing features by training this branch. Experiments on popular datasets [14, 15] show that the method proposed in this paper is competitive.

The contributions can be summarized as follows:

1. This paper uses IBN-Net as the backbone, complement the shortcomings of the IN and BN layers, and add spatial attention and channel attention to make the model pay more attention to person feature.
2. In order to be more applicable to the clothes-changing re-identification, this article adds the classification branch of the clothes to suppress the sensitivity of the model to the features of the clothes.
3. Wide experiments in this paper, not only experimented with commonly used data sets, but also experimented on a large-scale cross-space-time dataset, and all achieved good results.

2 Related Work

Person re-identification was first recognized as an independent task in the field of computer vision at the CVPR conference in 2006. In 2019, the task of clothes-changing (long-term) person re-identification was first proposed. At present, a large number of researchers have devoted themselves to the research of person re-identification algorithm technology without changing clothes, and have achieved very significant results. But there are few related studies, and the results are not ideal.

Traditional Person Re-identification. In recent years, person re-identification has developed rapidly. The research of person re-identification is divided into traditional methods and deep learning methods. The traditional methods [1, 2] mainly include two steps: feature extraction and similarity measurement. Discriminative and robust feature representation, such as color, HOG, SIFT, etc. The purpose of the similarity measure is to design the measure function as the intra-class distance is smaller, so that the inter-class distance is larger. For example, Kilian et al. [1] proposed to improve the nearest neighbor classification by learning the Mahalanobis distance measure. Liao et al. [2] proposed a subspace and metric learning method to make stable representations for viewpoint changes, and then obtain effective feature representations. However, traditional methods have limited learning ability and are difficult to adapt to tasks with large amounts of data. With the development of deep learning, the current work is mainly based on neural networks to learn discriminative features [3, 4, 6]. For example, Gong et al. [3] proposed a strategy to eliminate bias with bias to balance the weight between color features and color-independent features in the neural network by discarding part of the color information in the training data, thereby overcoming the effect of color segmentation. Sharma et al. [4] proposed a local-aware LA Transformer, which aggregates the globally enhanced local classification labels into a classifier set to improve the accuracy of person re-identification. Some studies have also proposed to integrate attention mechanisms into deep models, Xu et al. [6] added pose-guided part attention (PPA) and attention-aware feature synthesis (AFC) to the network to learn attention for rigid and non-rigid parts using pose information force mask, and then the global and partial features are embedded as the final feature. Li et al. [5] constructed a new Harmonious Attention CNN (HA-CNN) model for joint learning of soft pixel attention and hard region attention, while optimizing the feature representation, which can well solve the problem of misalignment of the input image. However, these works mainly focus on short-term Re-ID of color appearance-based features, which do not perform well in situations where persons change clothes.

Clothes-changing person re-identification. Currently, there are few studies on Re-ID [7, 8, 24, 25] for changing clothes, mainly from features that are not related to clothes from body shape, face or 3d shape. Wan et al. [7] focused on detecting facial information and extracting facial features to improve the accuracy of the model. Chen et al. [8] extracted texture-insensitive 3D shape embeddings directly from 2D images by adding 3D body reconstruction as an aid. However, most of these methods use auxiliary means, such as human skeleton, etc. Additional masks, pose or contour estimation increase the computational cost of these methods, and at the same time greatly increase the complexity of the model. Based on the above situation, this paper proposes an unassisted network used on RGB images, which learns the fine-grained features of the model through the attention mechanism, and uses the clothes classification branch to suppress the clothes features extracted by the network. The method is competitive with existing methods.

3 Method

Two parts are introduced in this section. In the first part, the overall structure of the network, backbone, attention module and branch module are introduced. In the second part, the loss functions used in the network are introduced.

3.1 Network

Overall Framework. The framework of this method is shown in Fig. 1. The backbone network adopts the IBN-Net with the last two layers removed, and then adds the channel and spatial attention modules to further capture the semantically related information of persons, suppress the influence of background information, and finally use MLP to classify the extracted person features. In order to make the model more suitable for changing clothes, a clothing classification branch is added to the person classification branch. The purpose is to obtain the parameters of the adversarial loss by classifying the clothes. In the process of minimizing the adversarial loss, the model is forced to learn non-clothing features.

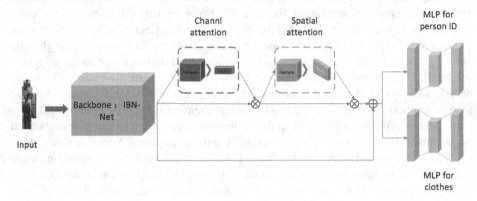

Fig. 1. The overall framework of the method

Backbone. Due to the change of different camera perspectives, the captured images of persons often have undesirable factors such as blur, occlusion, pose, color, style, and brightness, especially in changing clothes scenes, where the appearance of persons changes more.

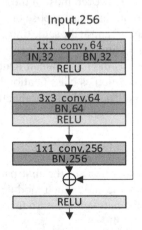

Fig. 2. IBN-Net residual block

In order to solve the above problems, this paper uses IBN-Net [9] as the backbone, and the network extracts the features of person images that do not change due to changes in appearance (style, color, and brightness, etc.) through the IN layer. And features such as person texture and contour are extracted through BN layer. The IBN-Net residual block is shown in Fig. 2.

Attention Module. The focus of person re-identification is the features related to persons, but there is often a large amount of background information in the captured person images, which greatly interferes with the re-identification task. In order to eliminate irrelevant background and better capture person features, this paper adds channel attention mechanism and spatial attention mechanism to the network [10].

The channel attention mechanism is designed to group and aggregate those semantically similar channels, allowing the network to pay more attention to person features and reduce the influence of background. The calculation method of channel attention is:

$$
\begin{aligned}
M_c(F) &= \sigma(\text{MLP}(\text{AvgPool}(F)) + \text{MLP}(\text{MaxPool}(F))) \\
&= \sigma\left(W_1\left(W_0\left(F_{avg}^c\right)\right) + W_1\left(W_0\left(F_{max}^c\right)\right)\right)
\end{aligned}
\tag{1}
$$

Among them, F is the extracted feature map, which σ is the activation function. In this paper, sigmoid is used as the activation function.

The spatial attention mechanism is used to capture and aggregate those semantically related pixels in the spatial domain, that is, to determine the pixel location of persons in space based on channel attention. Spatial attention is calculated as:

$$
\begin{aligned}
M_s(F) &= \sigma\left(f^{7\times7}\left(\left[\text{AvgPool}(F); \text{MaxPool}(F)\right]\right)\right) \\
&= \sigma\left(f^{7\times7}\left(\left[F_{avg}^s; F_{max}^s\right]\right)\right)
\end{aligned}
\tag{2}
$$

where f is the convolution operation, F and σ is the same as the definition in Eq. (1).

3.2 Loss Function

Loss Function of Clothes Classification Branch. In the clothing classification branch, this paper adopts the ASL classification loss [13], which can well balance the weight between positive and negative samples and solve the problem of labeling errors that may occur in clothing labeling. The ASL loss can be expressed as:

$$
ASL = \begin{cases} (1-p)^{\gamma_+} \log(p), \text{ positive} \\ (p)^{\gamma_-} \log(1-p), \text{ negative} \end{cases}
\tag{3}
$$

Among them, γ is the focus parameter, which is set γ_+ to 0 and γ_- to 4 in this article. p is the probability of each class output by the model and can be expressed as:

$$
p = \frac{e^{(f(x)_k)}}{\sum_{i=1}^{N} e^{(f(x)_i)}}, k \in S_{clo}
\tag{4}
$$

Among them, N is the number of categories of clothes, which $f(x)$ represents the feature vector obtained by the clothes classification branch, and k represents the kth clothes category.

Loss Function of Person Classification Branch. In person classification, we jointly use the label smooth loss [11] commonly used in representation learning, the triplet loss [12] commonly used in metric learning, and an adversarial loss to suppress the model's sensitivity to clothing features.

The label smooth loss can be expressed as:

$$L_{id} = -\sum_{i=1}^{N} p_i \log(p_i) \tag{5}$$

$$p_i = \begin{cases} 1 - \frac{N-1}{N}\varepsilon, & i = y \\ \frac{\varepsilon}{N}, & \text{otherwise} \end{cases} \tag{6}$$

Among them, N is the number of persons in the training set, p_i is the predicted probability of the output person identity, and y represents the real signature information of the person identity. Equation (6) represents the label smoothing operation, which ε is a hyperparameter with a small value. In this paper, let $= \varepsilon$ 0.1.

Triplet loss can be expressed as:

$$L = \max(d(a, p) - d(a, n) + \text{margin}, 0) \tag{7}$$

a is the anchor example, which p means that and a is a sample of the same category, and n that and a is a sample of a different category, and margin is a hyperparameter greater than 0. In this paper, the margin is set to 0.3. The final optimization goal is to narrow a the distance of the a sum and n the p distance of the farther.

In order to make the model pay more attention to non-clothing features, on the basis of the above two losses, this paper adds a clothing adversarial loss. In the person classification branch, the model has increased the distance between person features with different ids, but also increased the distance between the same person features that have changed clothes. The purpose of adding adversarial loss is to make people with the same identity but the same Persons changing clothes are closer. This paper further divides the clothes classification. On the basis of the original clothes classification, the clothes belonging to the same person in the data set are classified as positive samples, and the others are negative samples. The purpose is to make the clothes classification model unable to distinguish between people with the same id but wearing different clothes. Sample. The adversarial loss can be formulated as:

$$L_A = \begin{cases} \frac{1}{N_{S_{clo}^+}} \sum_{i=1}^{N_{S_{clo}^+}} (1 - p^+)^{\gamma^+} \log(p^+), & \text{positive} \\ \frac{\varepsilon}{N_{S_{clo}^-}} \sum_{i=1}^{N_{S_{clo}^-}} (p^-)^{\gamma^-} \log(1 - p^-), & \text{negative} \end{cases} \tag{8}$$

where $N_{S_{clo}^+}$ is the number of positive samples and is the number $N_{S_{clo}^-}$ of negative samples. For example, if a person has 10 sets of clothes, these 10 sets of clothes are positive samples, and the rest of the clothes are negative samples.

p^+ Represents the probability of a positive sample, which can be expressed as:

$$p^+ = \frac{e^{(f(x)_k)}}{e^{(f(x)_k)} + \sum_{i=1}^{N_{S_{clo}^-}} e^{(f(x)_i)}}, k \in S_{clo}^+ \tag{9}$$

p^- Represents the probability of a negative sample, which can be expressed as:

$$p^- = \frac{e^{(f(x)_k)}}{\sum_{i=1}^{N} e^{(f(x)_i)}}, k \in S_{clo}^- \tag{10}$$

where N is the total clothes types.

Then the total loss function can be expressed as:

$$L_{total} = L_{id} + \beta L_{triplet} + L_A \tag{11}$$

where β is a hyperparameter, set to 0.1 in this paper.

4 Experiments

4.1 Dataset

Verifies the effectiveness of the proposed algorithm on the popular clothing-changing person re-identification datasets PRCC [14] and Last [15].

PRCC is a dataset for person re-identification made public in 2020, consisting of 221 person identities and three camera views. The images in the PRCC dataset include multiple variations, such as changes in clothing, lighting, occlusion, pose, and perspective. There are 50 images of each person in the view of each camera, and approximately 152 images of each person are included in the dataset, for a total of 33,698 image.

LaST is a large-scale spatiotemporal person re-identification dataset for person re-identification released in 2021, including 10,862 person identities and more than 228,156 images. Compared with the existing datasets, LaST is more challenging and diverse, including from children to the elderly over 70 years old in the age dimension; in the time dimension including different time periods from day to night, persons can walk in space. Appearing in different cities in different countries, 76% of them changed their clothes.

4.2 Experimental Details

The operating system of the experimental platform is Ubuntu16.04, using two NVIDIA 2080TI GPUs, each with 12GB of video memory. The entire network is built in the Pytorch framework, and the batch size is set to 32. Each batch contains 8 persons, and each person contains 4 images. The input image is resized to 384 × 192. Random horizontal flip, random crop, and random wipe are used for data augmentation. The model was trained by Adam [27] for 60 epochs, and the learning rate was initially set to 3.5e–4, divided by 10 every 20 epochs.

4.3 Experimental Results

This paper compares with popular methods on PRCC and LaST datasets, and the comparison results are shown in the Table 1 and Table 2.

Table 1. Comparison with other popular methods on PRCC dataset

Methods	Time	PRCC			
		Cloth-changing		Same-cloth	
		Rank-1	mAP	Rank-1	mAP
HACNN16	2018	21.81	–	82.45	–
GI-ReID17	2022	33.3	–	80.0	–
ISP18	2020	36.6	–	92.8	–
RGA-SC19	2020	42.3	–	98.4	–
RCSANet 20	2021	50.2	48.6	100	97.2
3DSL 8	2021	51.3	–	–	–
Ours	2022	51.8	52.4	100	99.9

Table 2. Comparison with other popular methods on LaST dataset

Methods	Time	LaST		
		Rank-1	Rank-5	mAP
PCB21	2018	50.6	68.0	15.2
ABD-Net22	2019	48.5	67.6	16.1
QAConv23	2020	64.6	82.4	22.4
HOReID24	2020	68.3	82.3	25.5
Ours	2022	68.5	80.9	23.6

As shown in the tables, on PRCC dataset, our method outperforms methods such as RCSANet [19], 3DSL [8], etc. on Rank-1 and mAP metrics. And the method in this paper does not use the assistance of other modal data, and the model complexity is lower. Our method is also competitive on the LaST dataset, outperforming HOReID [23] on the Rank - 1 metric. In both datasets, the method in this paper achieves excellent performance, which verifies the effectiveness of the method and can be applied to the scene of re-identification of changing persons.

4.4 Visual Analysis

In this paper, the heat map is used to visualize the attention of different models to the person image area. As shown in Fig. 3, the first column is the original person image, the second column is the visualization heat map using only IBN-Net, and the third column is the method proposed in this paper. A visual heatmap of. As can be seen from Fig. 3, compared with the baseline, the model in this paper pays more attention to the body area and has a wider range of attention, and the feature maps mainly focus on body features that are not related to clothing, such as shoulders, body shape, and posture. Therefore, the method in this paper is more suitable for person re-identification of changing clothes.

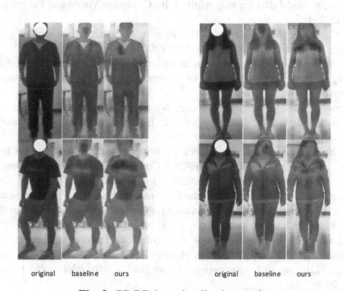

original   baseline   ours   original   baseline   ours

Fig. 3. PRCC data visualization results

5   Conclusion

The dual-branch network changing person re-identification method with attention mechanism proposed in this paper uses the pre-trained IBN-Net as the backbone network, and then completes feature extraction through channel attention and spatial attention modules, and then classify persons and clothes through the classification of persons and clothes. Double branches to suppress the network's extraction of clothing features. The method in this paper does not use the auxiliary means of other modalities, and the model is more lightweight. The network structure of this paper can well capture the inherent characteristics of clothes-clothing persons, and the final network can better mine non-clothing features from images, and can cope with the re-identification scene of clothes-changing persons. The superiority and robustness of our method are verified by experiments on two popular person Re-ID datasets and comparison with existing popular methods.

References

1. Weinberger, K.Q., Saul, L.K.: Fast solvers and efficient implementations for distance metric learning. In: Proceedings of the 25th International Conference on Machine Learning, pp. 1160–1167 (2008)
2. Liao, S., Hu, Y., Zhu, X., Li, S.Z.: Person re-identification by local maximal occurrence representation and metric learning. In: Proceedings of the IEEE Conference on Computer Vision and Pattern Recognition, pp. 2197–2206 (2015)
3. Gong, Y., Huang, L., Chen, L.: Eliminate deviation with deviation for data augmentation and a general multi-modal data learning method. In: Computer Vision and Pattern Recognition, pp. 1–12 (2021)
4. Sharma, C., Kapil, S.R., Chapman, D.: Person re-identification with a locally aware transformer. arXiv preprint arXiv:2106.03720 (2021)
5. Li, W., Zhu, X., Gong, S.: Harmonious attention network for person re-identification. In: Proceedings of the IEEE Conference on Computer Vision and Pattern Recognition, pp. 2285–2294 (2018)
6. Xu, J., Zhao, R., Zhu, F., Wang, H., Ouyang, W.: Attention-aware compositional network for person re-identification. In: Proceedings of the IEEE Conference on Computer Vision and Pattern Recognition, pp. 2119–2128 (2018)
7. Wan, F., Wu, Y., Qian, X., Chen, Y., Fu, Y.: When person re-identification meets changing clothes. In: Proceedings of the IEEE/CVF Conference on Computer Vision and Pattern Recognition Workshops, pp. 830–831 (2020)
8. Chen, J., et al.: Learning 3d shape feature for texture-insensitive person re-identification. In: Proceedings of the IEEE/CVF Conference on Computer Vision and Pattern Recognition, pp. 8146–8155 (2021)
9. Pan, X., Luo, P., Shi, J., Tang, X.: Two at once: enhancing learning and generalization capacities via IBN-Net. In: Ferrari, V., Hebert, M., Sminchisescu, C., Weiss, Y. (eds.) ECCV 2018. LNCS, vol. 11208, pp. 484–500. Springer, Cham (2018). https://doi.org/10.1007/978-3-030-01225-0_29
10. Woo, S., Park, J., Lee, J.-Y., Kweon, I.S.: CBAM: convolutional block attention module. In: Ferrari, V., Hebert, M., Sminchisescu, C., Weiss, Y. (eds.) ECCV 2018. LNCS, vol. 11211, pp. 3–19. Springer, Cham (2018). https://doi.org/10.1007/978-3-030-01234-2_1
11. Szegedy, C., Vanhoucke, V., Ioffe, S., Shlens, J., Wojna, Z.: Rethinking the Inception Architecture for Computer Vision. [online] Arxiv. Org (2018)
12. Zhai, Y., Guo, X., Lu, Y., Li, H.: In defense of the classification loss for person re-identification. In: Proceedings of the IEEE/CVF Conference on Computer Vision and Pattern Recognition Workshops (2019)
13. Ben-Baruch, E., et al.: Asymmetric loss for multi-label classification. arXiv preprint arXiv: 2009.14119 (2020)

14. Yang, Q., Wu, A., Zheng, W.S.: Person re-identification by contour sketch under moderate clothing change. IEEE Trans. Pattern Anal. Mach. Intell. **43**(6), 2029–2046 (2019)
15. Shu, X., et al.: Large-scale spatio-temporal person re-identification: algorithms and benchmark. IEEE Trans. Circ. Syst. Video Technol. (2021)
16. Jin, X., et al.: Cloth-changing person re-identification from a single image with gait prediction and regularization. In: Proceedings of the IEEE/CVF Conference on Computer Vision and Pattern Recognition, pp. 14278–14287 (2022)
17. Zhu, K., Guo, H., Liu, Z., Tang, M., Wang, J.: Identity-guided human semantic parsing for person re-identification. In: Vedaldi, A., Bischof, H., Brox, T., Frahm, J.-M. (eds.) ECCV 2020. LNCS, vol. 12348, pp. 346–363. Springer, Cham (2020). https://doi.org/10.1007/978-3-030-58580-8_21
18. Zhang, Z., Lan, C., Zeng, W., Jin, X., Chen, Z.: Relation-aware global attention for person re-identification. In: Proceedings of the IEEE/CVF Conference on Computer Vision and Pattern Recognition, pp. 3186–3195 (2020)
19. Huang, Y., Wu, Q., Xu, J., Zhong, Y., Zhang, Z.: Clothing status awareness for long-term person re-identification. In: Proceedings of the IEEE/CVF International Conference on Computer Vision, pp. 11895–11904 (2021)
20. Sun, Y., Zheng, L., Yang, Y., Tian, Q., Wang, S.: Beyond part models: person retrieval with refined part pooling (and a strong convolutional baseline). In: Ferrari, V., Hebert, M., Sminchisescu, C., Weiss, Y. (eds.) ECCV 2018. LNCS, vol. 11208, pp. 501–518. Springer, Cham (2018). https://doi.org/10.1007/978-3-030-01225-0_30
21. Chen, T., et al.: Abd-net: attentive but diverse person re-identification. In: Proceedings of the IEEE/CVF International Conference on Computer Vision, pp. 8351–8361 (2019)
22. Liao, S., Shao, L.: Interpretable and generalizable person re-identification with query-adaptive convolution and temporal lifting. In: Vedaldi, A., Bischof, H., Brox, T., Frahm, J.-M. (eds.) ECCV 2020. LNCS, vol. 12356, pp. 456–474. Springer, Cham (2020). https://doi.org/10.1007/978-3-030-58621-8_27
23. Wang, G.A., et al.: High-order information matters: Learning relation and topology for occluded person re-identification. In: Proceedings of the IEEE/CVF Conference on Computer Vision and Pattern Recognition, pp. 6449–6458 (2020)
24. Qian, X., et al.: Long-term cloth-changing person re-identification. In: Proceedings of the Asian Conference on Computer Vision (2020)
25. Chao, H., He, Y., Zhang, J., Feng, J.: Gaitset: regarding gait as a set for cross-view gait recognition. In: Proceedings of the AAAI Conference on Artificial intelligence, vol. 33, no. 01, pp. 8126–8133 (2019)
26. Ioffe, S., Szegedy, C.: Batch normalization: accelerating deep network training by reducing internal covariate shift. In: International Conference on Machine Learning, pp. 448–456. PMLR (2015)
27. Kingma, D.P., Ba, J.: Adam: A method for stochastic optimization. arXiv preprint arXiv:1412.6980 (2014)

Infant Cry Classification Based-On Feature Fusion and Mel-Spectrogram Decomposition with CNNs

Chunyan Ji[1] (ID), Yang Jiao[2] (ID), Ming Chen[3(✉)] (ID), and Yi Pan[2(✉)] (ID)

[1] Computer Science Department, BNU-HKBU United International College, Zhuhai, China
[2] Shenzhen Institute of Advanced Technology, Chinese Academy of Sciences, Shenzhen, China
yi.pan@siat.ac.cn
[3] College of Information Science and Engineering, Hunan Normal University, Changsha, China
chenming@hunnu.edu.cn

Abstract. We propose a novel method of using feature fusion and model fusion to improve infant cry classification performance. Spectrogram features extracted from transfer learning convolutional neural network model and mel-spectrogram features extracted from mel-spectrogram decomposition model are fused and fed into a multiple layer perception for better classification accuracy. The mel-spectrogram decomposition method feeds band-wise crops of the mel-spectrograms into multiple CNNs followed by a merged global classifier to capture more enhanced discriminative features. Feature fusion brings higher dimensional detailed information and characteristics more in line with human hearing perception together to achieve better performance on CNNs. The evaluation of the approach is conducted on Baby Chillanto database and Baby2020 database. Our approach yields a significant reduction of 4.72% absolute classification error rate compared with the result using single mel-spectrogram images with CNN model on Baby Chillanto database and our testing accuracy reaches 99.26%, which outperforms all other methods with this five-category classification task. The gender classification experiment on Baby2020 database also shows 3.87% accuracy improvement compared with the CNN model using single spectrograms.

Keywords: Infant cry classification · Mel-spectrogram decomposition · Feature fusion · Convolutional neural networks

1 Introduction

Infant cry research usually starts with data acquisition and preprocessing, followed by feature extraction and feature selection, and finally the classification model. To classify or detect certain types of cry signals, researchers have been using many types of features in the past decades for infant cry detection and classification. The commonly used features include cepstral domain features such as mel-frequency cepstral coefficient (MFCC) [1], linear prediction cepstral coefficients (LPCC) and bark frequency cepstral coefficients (BFCC) [2], prosodic features such as F0, formants, intensity [3], and image-based features such as spectrograms [4], waveforms [5], and mel-spectrograms [6]. Spectrograms are widely used in neural network models such as transformer model [7], Siamese neural network for animal audio classification [8], convolutional neural network (CNN) [9] for environmental sound classification, CNN models for infant cry classification [10]. Many successful works are performed using mel-spectrograms on audio research such as an augmentation technique on sequence-to-sequence voice conversion [11] and producing high quality speech synthesis [12].

SubspectralNet was proposed in [13] and it feeds band-wise crops of the mel-spectrograms into multiple CNN models followed by a merged global classifier to capture more enhanced discriminative features on acoustic scene classification. Zhang et al. further segmented the mel-spectrogram in both time and frequency dimension and proposed the mel-spectrogram decomposition model to further improve the performance of acoustic scene classification [14].

Feature fusion, the combination of features from different layers or branches, is an omnipresent part of modern network architectures [15]. It is used in image segmentation [16], image classification [15], audio-visual speech enhancement [17], and audio event classification [18], etc. In infant cry research, MFCC and prosodic features are fused for an FFNN for asphyxiated cry identification [19]. Cry signal spectrogram features and environmental features are fused to improve infant cry reason classification in a day care environment [20]. In this study, we propose an approach to fuse the features extracted from spectrograms and mel-spectrograms. We use transfer learning model to extract spectrogram features and use mel-spectrogram decomposition multi-CNN merging model to extract mel-spectrogram features. The multiple layer perception (MLP) classifier using fused features produces better overall classification accuracy.

In this paper, our major contributions include:

- We apply mel-spectrogram decomposition with multiple CNNs and model merging method onto infant cry classification to improve the classification accuracy.
- We propose to fuse spectrogram features and mel-spectrogram features to obtain more discriminative features of infant cry signals, as well as keeping the coverage of crying characteristics.
- Transfer learning CNN captures the high-level features of the spectrograms and mel-spectrogram decomposition makes local features more prominent. Fusing features from these two CNN feature extractors generates more thorough features of the original signals.

The remainder of the paper is organized as follows. In Sect. 2, spectrograms and mel-spectrograms are introduced and compared in detail. Section 3 describes our proposed feature fusion method and the details of the mel-spectrogram decomposition and model merging architecture. In Sect. 4, experimental results on infant cry type classification and infant gender classification are presented, and we conclude in Sect. 5.

2   Spectrograms vs. Mel-Spectrograms

A spectrogram is a visual representation of a signal at different frequencies as it varies with time. It is a two-dimensional heat map, in which the X-axis is the time, the Y-axis is the frequency, and the brightness of the color indicates the strength of the signal at a certain time and frequency. Spectrograms are extensively used in the field of speech, music, and animal sound, etc. A spectrogram can be obtained through four steps: framing, windowing, fast Fourier transform (FFT), and stacking the results of each frame. Framing is to divide the original signal into certain number of frames with a length, an overlap, and a framing hop. Hamming or other windowing is commonly used to avoid spectral leakage. The FFT converts the signal from the time domain to the frequency domain. Stacking up the result of FFT of each frame produces the spectrogram of a certain audio signal. A mel-spectrogram is another visual representation of a signal indicating how people hear sound by converting the Y-axis to mel-scale. Mel-spectrograms can relatively represent human sound perception characteristics, which presents the linear distribution under the 1000 Hz and the logarithm growth above the 1000 Hz on a logarithmic scale rather than a linear scale. People are more sensitive to lower frequency sound and the difference between high frequency sound is not as easy to distinguish as the ones between lower frequency sound. After framing, windowing, and FFT, frequency portion of the spectrogram is mapped to the mel scale perceptual filter bank using M triangular-shaped filter bank equally spaced on the mel range of frequency. The relationship between frequencies f and mel frequency scale is shown in (1):

$$M(f) = 2595 * log\left(1 + \frac{f}{700}\right) \tag{1}$$

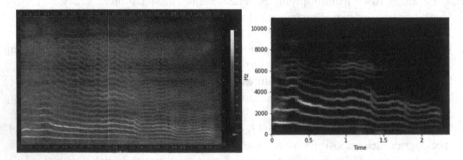

Fig. 1. The spectrogram (left) and the mel-spectrogram (right) of a hungry cry.

Figure 1 shows a hungry cry in spectrogram and mel-spectrogram. Comparing to mel-spectrogram, spectrogram contains higher dimensional features extracted from each frame of the signal, hence, the image contains more details, but some detailed information may not be necessarily useful for certain classification tasks. Mel-spectrogram is generated by adding filter banks on the mapping step and the commonly used filter banks are the same area triangular filter banks, which reduces higher frequency information more and the result is more in line with human hearing perception. As Fig. 1 illustrates, the higher frequency information on the mel-spectrogram is weakened and the mel-spectrogram has a lower dimension of features and carries less information, but certain frequency resolution is enhanced. The harmonic structure becomes drastically weaker as the frequency increases. Figure 2 illustrates the spectrograms and mel-spectrograms of an adult speech, an infant hungry cry, and a cat meow sound. We can see the differences among these three types of sound: (1) the speech contains obvious changes in vocal tract and the vibration of the vocal cords, producing unvoiced and voiced sounds to form meaningful speech; (2) the acoustic event such as cat meow sound can be clearly seen that there is no articulation ability and no control in breathing, which is shown as a flat bar in the spectrogram without pause or changes of inspiration and expiration phases; (3) the spectrogram of an infant cry is likely in between the speech signal and cat sound signal. It is more stationary compared to human speech while includes more changes of inspiration and expiration with respect to live animal sound. As mel-spectrograms are more suitable for speech recognition since it is more in line with human hearing perception, the spectrograms contain more information for other acoustic scene sounds including animal sounds. Combining spectrogram features and mel-spectrogram features can cover a wider range of diversity of changes within infant cry signals leading to robust classification performance for CNNs.

3   Model Architecture

As shown in Fig. 3, our proposed method involves spectrogram feature extraction from transfer learning model, mel-spectrogram feature extraction from mel-spectrogram decomposition model, feature fusion, and MLP. Given a set of wav files $W = (W_1, W_2, \ldots W_n)$, corresponding spectrograms and mel-spectrograms are generated using Sox [21] and librosa [22] software, respectively. The generated images are resized into the appropriate size as model input for the following two feature extractors.

3.1   Spectrogram Feature Extractor

The spectrogram extractor is built using a ResNet50 based transfer learning CNN model. The layers before the fully connected layer in ResNet50 are saved as the base model and custom layers are appended after the base model. All spectrograms are separated using the 5-fold validation method and the trained model is used to extract the feature vectors of the testing set. Spectrogram features $S = (S_1, S_2, \ldots S_n)$ is extracted from the last fully connected layer.

3.2   Mel-Spectrogram Feature Extractor

Each mel-spectrogram is decomposed equally into 4 sub mel-spectrograms horizontally, which contains 32 mel-bins in each slice. We denote the set of the 4 sub mel-spectrograms as $M^i = (M_1^i, M_2^i, \ldots M_n^i)$ where $i \in \{1, 2, 3, 4\}$. We choose to decompose the mel-spectrogram into 4 slices based on the experimental results, which show that 4-slice or 5-slice method outperforms the 2, 3, 6, or 7 slices. $M^i = (M_1^i, M_2^i, \ldots M_n^i)$ is the input for $(CNN)^i$, each of which contains a convolutional layer, a max pooling, a flattened layer, and a dense layer. The outputs of $(CNN)^i$ are concatenated and followed by a dense layer and a softmax layer for classification. The mel-spectrogram extractor model is trained on 80% samples and features from the last dense layer are extracted as the mel-spectrogram features denoted as $M = (M_1, M_2, \ldots M_n)$. The loss function used in

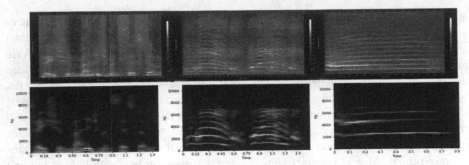

Fig. 2. Spectrograms (top row) and mel-spectrograms (bottom row) of adult speech (left), infant cry (middle), and cat meow sound (right).

$(CNN)^i$ and the merged model is categorical cross entropy as shown in (2) and the Adam optimizer is applied.

$$Loss = -\sum\nolimits_{k=1}^{n} y_k * log\widehat{y_k} \tag{2}$$

$S = (S_1, S_2, \ldots S_n)$ and $M = (M_1, M_2, \ldots M_n)$ are then concatenated to be the new feature vector, $Zconcat = S||M$ where S denotes the spectrogram features and M denotes the mel-spectrogram features, as the input of a MLP model, which is trained separately from the extractors. The last layer of the MLP is a softmax function classifying different types of cry samples.

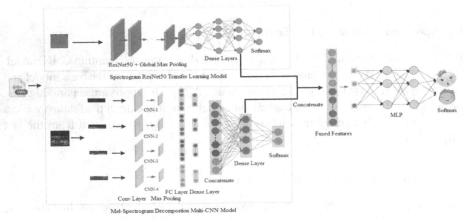

Fig. 3. Model architecture of our feature fusion approach.

4 Experimental Setup and Results

4.1 Datasets

We evaluate the effectiveness of the approach on two datasets. They are a subset of our developing Baby2020 database and Baby Chillanto database. Baby2020 samples are collected from over 100 babies from newborn to 9 months old via mobile devices placed right beside the infants in natural real-world home or hospital environments. The length of each recording is less than 3 min with 16 kHz sample rate. Cry samples are manually segmented with the length between 1 s to 7 s. In this study, we use 4000 cry samples from Baby2020, including 2000 cries from baby boy younger than 3 months and 2000 cries from baby girl younger than 3 months. Baby Chillanto database was collected by National Institute of Astrophysics and Optical Electronics, CONACYT Mexico [23]. The cries are recorded by doctors from babies ranging from newborn to 9-month of age and each sample is a one-second-long audio wav file. In this study, we use 340 asphyxia samples, 879 deaf samples, 350 hunger samples, 506 normal cries, and 192 pain cries.

4.2 Experimental Setup

Sound eXchange (Sox) [21] is used to generate spectrograms from the wav files. In the spectrogram feature extractor, the spectrograms are in size 256×256 for Chillanto dabase and 128×128 for Baby2020 database due to the size of the datasets. From the trained ResNet50, we take the convolutional layers before the fully connect 1000 layer as the base model. The custom layers appended to the base model contains a GlobalMaxPooling layer, one 1024-neuron dense layer, a 512-neuron dense layer, a dropout layer with a rate of 0.25, and another 32-neuron dense layer. The transfer learning CNN model is trained on 80% of samples and used to extract the features for the rest of the 20% testing samples. After five round of training and extracting, the features for all samples are extracted and are combined to be a $n \times 32$ matrix feature vector, where n is the number of samples.

The mel-spectrogram is extracted using librosa [22] with 2048 FFT points, 128 mel-bins, and a hop-length of 256. The sampling rate used is the original one from the cry samples, which is 16K for Baby2020 cries, 11250, 8000, 22050 for Baby Chillanto asphyxia, deaf and hunger, normal and pain, respectively. The amplitude of the mel-spectrogram is scaled logarithmically. The scaled mel-spectrogram is decomposed into 4 slices equally and they are resized to 35×50 (height $\times$ width) to fit the CNN model input size. Each CNN for each slice has the same architecture, which contains a convolutional layer with twenty 5×5 filters followed by a max-pooling layer, which uses 2×2 filter with stride 2. Then there is a flatten layer and a dense layer with 128 neurons. The output of each CNN is concatenated appended by one 64 neuron dense layer and a 32-neuron dense layer with ReLu activation function, at last a softmax activation function is applied to the last dense layer for classification. We use this mel-spectrogram decomposition and merged model to extract mel-spectrogram features. The 32 features in the last dense layer are extracted and concatenated to the 32 features from spectrogram extractor. The fused features are then input into an MLP, which is written in Pytorch containing four hidden layers with 1056, 512, 256, 64 neurons, respectively. The optimizer used is Adam and the learning rate is set to 0.001 and the activation function for the output layer is softmax.

4.3 Results and Analysis

The two experiments designed to evaluate the approach are infant cry reason classification and gender classification. Many previous research has classified the infant cry reason with good accuracy and we hope to further improve the performance. Gender classification is specifically designed for this approach to show that our proposed method is also effective on all healthy cry samples with precise labels.

Spectrograms are used in other related studies for infant cry classification on Baby Chillanto database. As shown in Table 1, the five-category classification reaches 90.08% using spectrograms in transfer learning method. Using Mel-spectrograms as feature input, the accuracy of a simple CNN model reaches 94.54%, which outperforms the best model using spectrograms. Mel-spectrogram decomposition method improves the accuracy up to 98.70% and our proposed fusion method reaches 99.26%. In [13], authors show that depending on the scene class, there is a specific frequency band showing most activity, hence providing discriminative features for that class. We believe the reason of that mel-spectrogram decomposition also performs well in Baby Chillanto database is because the five types of cries include both healthy cries and pathological cries, which contain discriminative features in different bands. In the gender classification experiment, mel-spectrogram decomposition method is also powerful. As shown on Table 2, our proposed fusion method yields 3.87% accuracy improvement compared with the CNN model using single spectrograms and the result outperforms all other types of single feature methods. Our proposed fusion method combines high-level global features and detailed local features of sub bands, and improves the discriminative ability of the final classifier.

Table 1. Experimental results on baby chillanto database.

Features	Model	Accuracy
Spectrograms	CNN	87.03%
Spectrograms	Resnet50 transfer learning (TLCNN)	90.08%
Mel-spectrograms	CNN	94.54%
Mel-spectrograms	Decomposition 4-CNN	98.70%
Spectrograms + Mel-spectrograms	TLCNN + Decomposition 4-CNN + MLP	99.26%

Table 2. Experimental results on Baby2020 database.

Features	Model	Accuracy
Spectrograms	CNN	92.77%
Spectrograms	Resnet50 Transfer Learning (TLCNN)	94.84%
Mel-spectrograms	CNN	90.26%
Mel-spectrograms	Decomposition 4-CNN	93.15%
Spectrograms + Mel-spectrograms	TLCNN + Decomposition 4-CNN + MLP	96.64%

5   Conclusion

In this paper, we demonstrated that mel-spectrogram decomposition is effective on infant cry classification and fusing spectrogram features and mel-spectrogram feature can further improve classification performance. Transfer learning CNN captures the high-level features of the spectrograms and mel-spectrogram decomposition extracts the detailed local features, and more thorough features of the original signals are generated by fusing these two types of features, which improves the final classification accuracy. Cry reason classification on Baby Chillanto database and gender classification on Baby2020 database were used to evaluate the proposed method. Our approach yields 4.72% accuracy improvement than the result using single mel-spectrograms with CNN model on Baby Chillanto database and our testing accuracy reaches 99.26%, which outperforms all other methods. The gender classification experiment on Baby2020 database also shows 3.87% accuracy improvement compared with the CNN model using single spectrograms. Although our method focuses on infant cry classification, it can be extended to other acoustic scene classification tasks or diagnosis of childhood diseases including autism [24].

Acknowledgement. This work was supported by BNU-HKBU United International College Start-up Research Fund (UICR0700051–23) and the Shenzhen KQTD Project (No. KQTD20200820113106007). We acknowledge Molecular Basis of Disease (MBD) at Georgia State University for the support. We thank Dr. Carlos A. Reyes-Garcia, Dr. Emilio Arch-Tirado and his INR-Mexico group, and Dr. Edgar M. Garcia-Tamayo for collecting the Infant Cry database. We also express our great gratitude to Dr. Orion Reyes and Dr. Carlos A. Reyes for providing the access to the Baby Chillanto database. We thank all parents, doctors, and nurses who support the recording of Baby2020 database.

References

1. Lavner, Y., Cohen, R., Ruinskiy, D., Ijzerman, H.: Baby cry detection in domestic environment using deep learning. In: 2016 IEEE International Conference on the Science of Electrical Engineering (ICSEE) (2017). https://doi.org/10.1109/ICSEE.2016.7806117
2. Liu, L., Li, Y., Kuo, K.: Infant cry signal detection, pattern extraction and recognition. In: 2018 International Conference on Information and Computer Technologies (ICICT), pp. 159–163. IEEE (2018). https://doi.org/10.1109/INFOCT.2018.8356861
3. Rosales-Pérez, A., Reyes-García, C.A., Gonzalez, J.A., Reyes-Galaviz, O.F., Escalante, H.J., Orlandi, S.: Classifying infant cry patterns by the genetic selection of a fuzzy model. Biomed. Signal Process. Control **17**, 38–46 (2015). https://doi.org/10.1016/j.bspc.2014.10.002
4. Franti, E., Ispas, I., Dascalu, M.: Testing the universal baby language hypothesis-automatic infant speech recognition with cnns. In: 2018 41st International Conference on Telecommunications and Signal Processing (TSP), pp. 1–4. IEEE (2018). https://doi.org/10.1109/TSP.2018.8441412
5. Sachin, M.U., Nagaraj, R., Samiksha, M., Rao, S., Moharir, M.: GPU based deep learning to detect asphyxia in neonates. Indian J. Sci. Technol. **10**(3) (2017). https://doi.org/10.17485/ijst/2017/v10i3/110617
6. Lim, H., Park, J., Lee, K., Han, Y.: Rare sound event detection using 1D convolutional recurrent neural networks. In: Dcase 2017 Proceeding, pp. 2–6 (2017)

7. Gong, Y., Chung, Y.A., Glass, J.: AST: Audio Spectrogram Transformer (2021). https://doi. org/10.21437/interspeech.2021-698
8. Nanni, L., Rigo, A., Lumini, A., Brahnam, S.: Spectrogram classification using dissimilarity space. Appl. Sci. **10**(12), 1–17 (2020). https://doi.org/10.3390/APP10124176
9. Palanisamy, K., Singhania, D., Yao, A.: Rethinking CNN Models for Audio Classification (2020). http://arxiv.org/abs/2007.11154
10. Chang, C.-Y., Tsai, L.-Y.: A CNN-based method for infant cry detection and recognition. In: Barolli, L., Takizawa, M., Xhafa, F., Enokido, T. (eds.) WAINA 2019. AISC, vol. 927, pp. 786–792. Springer, Cham (2019). https://doi.org/10.1007/978-3-030-15035-8_76
11. Hwang, Y., Cho, H., Yang, H., Won, D.O., Oh, I., Lee, S.W.: Mel-spectrogram augmentation for sequence-to-sequence voice conversion (2020). http://arxiv.org/abs/2001.01401
12. Juvela, L., Bollepalli, B., Yamagishi, J., Alku, P.: Gelp: GAN-excited linear prediction for speech synthesis from mel-spectrogram. In: Proceedings Annual Conference International Speech Communication Association. Interspeech, pp. 694–698 (2019). https://doi.org/10. 21437/Interspeech.2019-2008
13. Phaye, S.S.R., Benetos, E., Wang, Y.: Subspectralnet – Using Sub-Spectrogram Based Convolutional Neural Networks for Acoustic Scene ClassificatioN School of Computing , National University of Singapore, Singapore School of EECS , Queen Mary University of London , UK 3 The Alan Turing Institu, pp. 825–829 (2019)
14. Zhang, T., Feng, G., Liang, J., An, T.: Acoustic scene classification based on Mel spectrogram decomposition and model merging. Appl. Acoust. **182**, 108258 (2021). https://doi.org/10. 1016/j.apacoust.2021.108258
15. Dai, Y., Gieseke, F., Oehmcke, S., Wu, Y., Barnard, K.: Attentional Feature Fusion, pp. 3559–3568 (2021). https://doi.org/10.1109/wacv48630.2021.00360
16. Chen Y, et al.: Research of improving semantic image segmentation based on a feature fusion model. J. Ambient Intell. Hum. Comput. **9**, 1–3 (2020). https://doi.org/10.1007/s12652-020-02066-z
17. Xu, X., et al.: AMFFCN: Attentional Multi-layer Feature Fusion Convolution Network for Audio-visual Speech Enhancement (2021). http://arxiv.org/abs/2101.06268
18. McLoughlin, I., Xie, Z., Song, Y., Phan, H., Palaniappan, R.: Time–frequency feature fusion for noise robust audio event classification. Circuits Syst. Signal Process. **39**(3), 1672–1687 (2019). https://doi.org/10.1007/s00034-019-01203-0
19. Ji, C., Xiao, X., Basodi, S., Pan, Y.: Deep learning for asphyxiated infant cry classification based on acoustic features and weighted prosodic features. In: Proceedings 2019 IEEE International Congress Cybermatics 12th IEEE International Conference Internet Things, 15th IEEE International Conference Green Computing Communication 12th IEEE International Confernce Cybermatics Phys. So (2019). https://doi.org/10.1109/iThings/GreenCom/ CPSCom/SmartData.2019.00206
20. Chang, C.M., Chen, H.Y., Chen, H.C., Lee, C.C.: Sensing with contexts: crying reason classification for infant care center with environmental fusion. In: 2020 Asia-Pacific Signal and Information Processing Association Annual Summit and Conference (APSIPA ASC), pp. 314–318 (2020)
21. Sox Homepage. https://en.wikipedia.org/wiki/SoX
22. McFee, B., et al.: librosa: Audio and Music Signal Analysis in Python (2015). https://doi.org/ 10.25080/majora-7b98e3ed-003
23. Reyes-Galaviz, O.F., Cano-Ortiz, S.D., Reyes-García, C.A.: Evolutionary-neural system to classify infant cry units for pathologies identification in recently born babies. In: 2008 Seventh Mexican International Conference on Artificial Intelligence, pp. 330-335. IEEE (2008). https://doi.org/10.1109/MICAI.2008.73
24. Ma, R., Wang, Y., Wei, Y., Pan, Y.: Meta-data Study in Autism Spectrum Disorder Classification Based on Structural MRI (2022). arXiv preprint arXiv:2206.05052

Author Index

Printed in the United States
by Baker & Taylor Publisher Services